CAVE
LawCards

Family Law

Cavendish
Publishing
Limited

First published in Great Britain 1997 by Cavendish Publishing Limited, The Glass House, Wharton Street, London WC1X 9PX, United Kingdom.

Telephone: +44 (0) 171 278 8000 Facsimile: +44 (0) 171 278 8080

e-mail: info@cavendishpublishing.com

Visit our Home Page on http://www.cavendishpublishing.com

© Cavendish Publishing Limited 1997

Reprinted 1998

Lawcard on family law

1.Domestic relations - England 2.Domestic relations - England - Examinations, questions, etc.

I.Family Law

344.2'0615

ISBN 1 85941 326 9

Printed and bound in Great Britain

Contents

1 Nullity 1
    Void marriages 1
    Voidable marriages 5
    Wilful refusal 7
    Unsoundness of mind 8
    Duress 8
    Bars when marriages are voidable 10

2 Divorce 12
    Matrimonial Causes Act 1973 12
    Adultery and intolerability 12
    Behaviour 13
    Desertion 14
    Separation 16
    Consent 17
    Time requirements 17
    Reconciliation 18
    Provisions affecting the granting of decrees 18
    Wrong to dissolve the marriage 19

3 Ancillary relief 22
    The welfare of minor children of the family (s 25(1)) 22
    Financial resources (s 25(2)(a)) 22
    Financial obligations (s 25(2)(b)) 22
    Standard of living (s 25(2)(c)) 23
    Ages and duration of marriage (s 25(2)(d)) 23
    Cohabitation prior to marriage 24
    Physical or mental disability (s 25(2)(e)) 24
    Contribution to the family welfare (s 25(2)(f)) 24
    Conduct it would be inequitable to disregard (s 25(2)(g)) 24
    Loss of future benefit (s 25(2)(h)) 25

Clean break provisions (s 25(A))   25
Sections 23, 24, 24A: Financial orders   26
Property orders   27
Section 31 MCA: Variation of orders   28
Child Support Act 1991 (s 8(3))   30
Child Support Act and clean breaks   31
White Paper 1995: improving child support   32

4 Property rights and disputes between spouses and cohabitees   34
Married Women's Property Act 1882 (s 17)   34
How are s 17 MWPA decisions reached?   34
Interests in land   34
Resulting, implied or constructive trusts   35
Direct financial contributions   35

5 Domestic violence   43
Matrimonial Homes Act 1983   43
Applicants for MHA orders   43
Domestic violence and Matrimonial Proceedings Act 1976   46
Domestic proceedings and Magistrates' Court Act 1978   49
Factors to consider in DVMPA cases   50
Power of arrest   50
The inherent jurisdiction of the court   51
Undertakings   51

6 Children I   53
Children Act 1989   54
Welfare and delay principles   55
The new orders   56
Residence orders   58
Contact orders   60
Prohibited steps orders   62

Specific issues orders   63
Who can apply for s 8 orders?   64
Welfare principle in leave applications   65
When can children apply for s 8 orders?   66
Child applications for leave   66
Family assistance order   66
Private law   67
The ascertainable wishes and feelings of
    the child   68
The child's physical, emotional and educational needs   68
The likely effect on the child of any change in
    his or her circumstances   69
The capability of each parent of meeting the child's
    needs   70
Financial provisions and property adjustment
    for children   71
Guardianship   71
The revocation and disclaimer of an appointment   71

7 Children II   73
Care and supervision orders   73
How decisions on care orders will be reached   76
Appointment of a guardian *ad litem*   81
Child assessment order requirements   83
Wardship and the inherent jurisdiction   87
Wardship and the Children Act 1989   88
Wardship applications   89
Adoption   90
Who can apply?   93
Who can adopt   93
Parental agreement   94
Criteria for granting adoption order   94
Proposals for reform   98

8 Divorce reform 99

Criticisms of present system 99
Family Law Act 1996 101
Part I 101
Part II 102
Availability of divorce/separation orders 104
Irretrievable breakdown 106
Time periods to be met during DO/SO procedure 108
Exemptions to required arrangements for the future 111
Part III 116
Part IV 119
Effect of orders 122
Criteria for occupation order 124
Duration 127
Obligations courts may apply to occupation orders 128
Criteria for granting non-molestation orders 133

1 Nullity

Although less than 1% of marriages are now terminated by nullity petitions today, examiners still require a knowledge of this area.

Nullity falls into two categories – void and voidable marriages. Each area has its own concepts and grounds for its existence.

Void marriages

There are social and public policy reasons as to why the marriage should not exist, as illustrated by the grounds contained in s 11 Matrimonial Causes Act (MCA) 1973.

Marriages celebrated after 31 July 1971 shall be void on the following grounds:

Section 11(a)(i)

That the parties to the marriage are within the prohibited degrees of relationship; either blood relations (consanguinity) or non-blood relations (affinity).

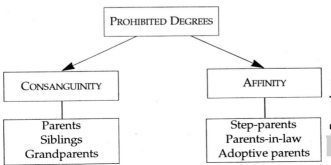

Section 11(a)(ii)

That either party is under the age of 16. However, if both parties are domiciled abroad at the time of the marriage it will be recognised as valid if the marriage is recognised as valid in the country in which it was celebrated.

If either party is aged over 16 but under 18 then consent is required from certain people:

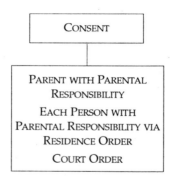

However, if this consent is lacking, the marriage will not be void unless the parents have publicly objected to the banns thereby voiding the banns. An application can also be made to the High Court, county court, or magistrates' court to obtain consent if consent cannot be obtained because of the parents' absence or inaccessibility.

Section 11(a)(iii)

That the parties have intermarried in disregard to certain requirements as to the formation of marriage.

Publicity has been deemed necessary to prevent clandestine marriages as is illustrated by the existing rules which are complex and dealt with here only in outline.

Church of England weddings

Formalities for weddings

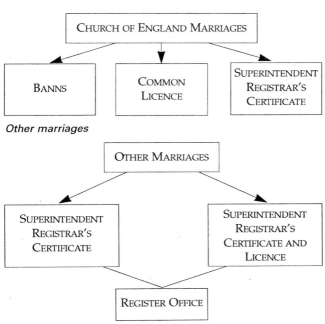

Other marriages

When there are defects in the formalities the marriage will only be void if they are done 'knowingly and wilfully' by both parties.

Section 11(b)

That at the time of the marriage either party was already lawfully married.

This section requires the parties to fulfil the definition of marriage contained in *Hyde v Hyde* (1866), ie 'The voluntary union for life of one man and one woman to the exclusion of all others'.

The case of *Maples v Maples* (1987) illustrates that if a party has entered a valid marriage then to terminate that marriage and be able to enter another the termination must also be valid.

Section 11(c)

That the parties are not respectively male and female.

The cases arising in this area normally concern a party who has undergone surgery for a sex change.

UK	EUROPE
Corbett v Corbett (1970)	*Rees v UK* (1990)
	Cossey v UK (1991)
	B v France (1992)

Section 11(d)

That in the case of a polygamous marriage entered into outside England and Wales that either party was at the time of the marriage domiciled in England or Wales.

In this situation a marriage is polygamous if it is actually polygamous or potentially polygamous.

Section 47 MCA allows matrimonial relief or a declaration concerning validity of a marriage entered into under a law allowing polygamy (matrimonial relief includes nullity, divorce, judicial separation and matters relating to maintenance provisions). However, there have been cases where s 11(d) has not applied.

In *Radwan v Radwan (No 2)* (1973) the husband was domiciled in Egypt and married his first wife, an Egyptian domiciled woman, in Cairo. He later married his second wife, an English domiciled woman in Paris intending to enter into a polygamous marriage according to Egyptian law and intending to live in Egypt. They did live in Egypt but later moved to, and became domiciled in, England. The second wife later petitioned for divorce.

The court held that as the second marriage was valid in Egypt and they had intended to live there it was valid in England. The court said s 11(d) did not apply.

In *Hussain v Hussain* (1982) even though there was a potentially polygamous marriage, both parties had no capacity to marry again and s 11(d) did not apply, so the marriage was valid.

Voidable marriages

Voidable marriages are defective, but it is for the parties involved to decide whether they will end the marriage. The marriage will continue until it is avoided by way of a decree.

Section 16 MCA 1973 says that a decree of nullity granted after 31 July 1971 on the ground that a marriage is voidable, will only annul the marriage with respect to any time after the decree has been made absolute and the marriage will be treated as it if had existed up to that time notwithstanding the decree.

When a voidable marriage ends

> *Ward v Secretary of State for Social Services* (1990)
>
> *Pike v Pike* (1994)

The grounds for marriages formed after 31 July 1971 being voidable are contained in s 12 MCA 1973.

Section 12(a)
That the marriage has not been consummated owing to the incapacity of either party to consummate it.

Section 12(b)
That the marriage has not been consummated owing to the wilful refusal of the respondent to consummate it.

The difference in the wording of these grounds shows that under s 12(a) a party can petition on his or her own incapacity but under s 12(b) cannot petition on his or her own wilful refusal.

Consummation occurs as soon as parties have sexual intercourse after the marriage. Sexual intercourse before marriage does not amount to consummation. The degree of sexual intercourse required was defined in *D v A* (1845).

Wilful refusal

This is defined in *Horton v Horton* (1947) as 'a settled and definite decision come to without just excuse'.

This can arise in a number of ways, such as a psychological problem which does not amount to incapacity and the refusal to undergo an operation to remedy a physical defect preventing consummation, but this must meet the definition, ie be a settled and definite decision without just cause.

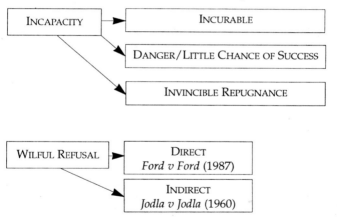

Section 12(c)

Lack of consent: that either party did not validly consent, whether in consequence of duress, mistake, unsoundness of mind or otherwise.

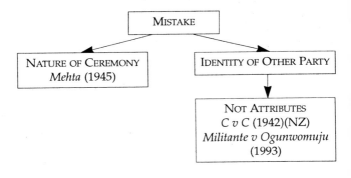

Unsoundness of mind

UNSOUNDNESS OF MIND
Failure to understand duties/responsibilities of marriage

There is a rebuttable presumption that once the marriage ceremony has been performed there has been valid consent by both parties: it is rare for this ground to succeed.

Duress

Duress is said to be fear which is so overbearing that the element of free consent is absent.

In *Szechter v Szechter* (1971) it was said that it must amount to:

> ... a genuine and reasonably held fear caused by the threat of immediate danger (for which the party himself if not responsible) to life, limb or liberty, so that the constraint destroys the reality of consent.

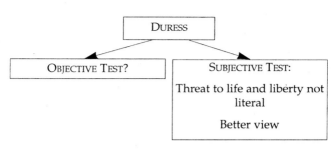

It is generally accepted that a subjective test is to be applied in this situation, ie 'has the petitioner been affected by the pressure?', not 'would an ordinary person of firm standing be affected?' (*Scott v Sebright* (1886)).

Section 12(d)

This section deals with a party suffering from a mental disorder. In this situation a party can give a valid consent and because of this the marriage cannot be avoided by s 12(c) but the party is not fit for marriage because of the mental disorder.

The mental disorder, which can be continuous or intermittent, must be within the Mental Health Act 1983.

Section 12(e)

That at the time of marriage the respondent was suffering from VD in a communicable form.

Section 12(f)

That at the time of the marriage the respondent was pregnant by some person other than the petitioner.

If the situation arises where the respondent wishes to prevent a decree of nullity being granted, the use of s 13 MCA 1973 must be considered.

Bars when marriages are voidable

These are contained in s 13 MCA 1973.

Section 13(1)
The court shall not grant a decree of nullity on the ground that a marriage is voidable if the respondent satisfies the court:

- That the petitioner, with knowledge that it was open to him to have the marriage avoided, so conducted himself in relation to the respondent as to lead the respondent reasonably to believe that he would not seek to do so.

- That it would be unjust to the respondent to grant the decree.

KNOWLEDGE : CONDUCT : UNJUST

Section 13(2) and (3)

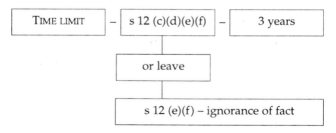

TIME LIMIT – s 12 (c)(d)(e)(f) – 3 years

or leave

s 12 (e)(f) – ignorance of fact

Section 13(4)
This allows leave to be granted for proceedings to be instituted out of time if the court:

- is satisfied the petitioner has at some time during that period suffered from a mental disorder within MHA 1983; and

- considers that in all the circumstances of the case it would be just to grant leave for the institution of proceedings.

2 Divorce

Matrimonial Causes Act 1973

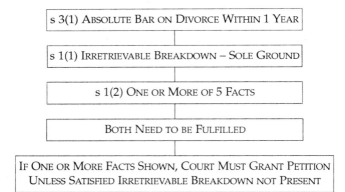

s 3(1) Absolute Bar on Divorce Within 1 Year

s 1(1) Irretrievable Breakdown – Sole Ground

s 1(2) One or More of 5 Facts

Both Need to be Fulfilled

If One or More Facts Shown, Court Must Grant Petition Unless Satisfied Irretrievable Breakdown not Present

Adultery and intolerability

Section 1(2)(a)
The elements of the definition of adultery must be known.

Adultery
Voluntary sexual intercourse between a married person and a person of the opposite sex, who may or may not be married and who is not the other person's spouse.

A person cannot commit adultery if they are insane and a wife has not committed adultery if she has been raped. It must be voluntary (*Redpath v Redpath and Milligan* (1950)).

The degree of sexual intercourse required for adultery is that some degree of penetration is achieved (*Dennis v Dennis*

(1955)). (This can be compared with the degree of sexual intercourse required for consummation, ie 'ordinary and complete'.)

Adultery is considered to be a serious matrimonial offence and as such a standard of proof higher than the normal civil standard of proof is required (*Bastable v Bastable* (1968)).

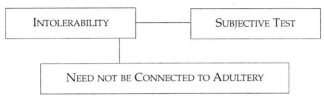

Reconciliation provision: s 2(1) and (2)
Cohabitation of over six months after becoming aware of adultery 'destroys' the fact.

Behaviour

Section 1(2)(b)
This fact is normally referred to as 'unreasonable behaviour'. However, the aspect of 'unreasonableness' must be considered in relation to whether or not the petitioner is expected to live with the respondent and not to the standard of behaviour.

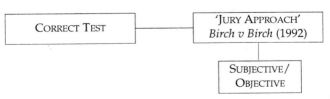

Reconciliation provions

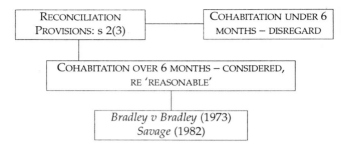

Desertion

Section 1(2)(c)

There are said to be four requirements to prove the fact of desertion. They are:

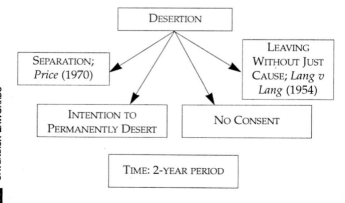

Termination of desertion
Absolute defences:

- The granting of a decree of judicial separation or a valid separation agreement. These are seen as supervening consent.

- The refusal of a reasonable offer of reconciliation without just cause, eg a party offering reconciliation but attaching unreasonable conditions, eg in *Hutchinson v Hutchinson* (1963) there was to be no sexual intercourse.

- Resumption of cohabitation would amount to returning to a state of affairs where desertion would not have been found originally.

Discretionary defences
- Petitioner's implied consent to the separation by taking action to prevent the other spouse returning.

- Petitioner unsuccessfully petitioning for divorce or nullity, on other grounds.

- Petitioner's own adultery unless respondent is indifferent to it.

Separation

Section 1(2)(d) – two years' separation and respondent consents.

Section 1(2)(e) – five years' separation.

The recognition of the marriage being at an end can be made unilaterally, and need not be communicated to the other spouse. It is clear that this could cause hardship and the court will require evidence showing when such a decision was reached. This could be by way of oral evidence, a letter or the ending of regular visits. However, if the court only has the oral evidence of the petitioner it will treat such evidence with caution and look at the surrounding circumstances to see if there are any other indications as to when the period began.

Separate households

Section 2(6) says that a husband and wife shall be treated as living apart unless they are living with each other in the same household. This means that we have to consider the question of separate households under the same roof.

The essential element is that it can be shown that there has been a change in the nature of the relationship. This can best be illustrated by comparing the cases of *Fuller v Fuller* (1973) and *Mouncer v Mouncer* (1972).

Consent

The essential difference in these facts concerns the requirement of consent by the respondent in s 1(2)(d) only.

The petitioner has the burden of showing that the respondent has consented in the proper manner. This consent must be express and is normally given via a signed statement. The respondent should be given sufficient information to enable him to give a proper consent to the decree.

The court will not imply any element of consent (*McGill v Robson* (1972)).

As with all matters of consent there must be capacity (*Mason v Mason* (1972)). Again it is for the petitioner to show that the respondent has this capacity if there is any doubt.

The respondent can withdraw his consent at any time prior to the decree nisi (r 16(2) Matrimonial Causes Rules 1977). Also under s 10(1) MCA 1973 the respondent may apply to the court any time before decree absolute for the decree nisi to be rescinded if he can satisfy the court that he was misled by the petitioner, whether intentionally or not, on any matter which he took into consideration in giving his consent.

Time requirements

These are strictly applied as shown by *Warr v Warr* (1975) and do not include the day of separation.

In s 1(2)(e) cases, once the period of five years has been shown to exist then the respondent cannot be granted a decree (*Parsons v Parsons* (1975)).

Reconciliation

RECONCILIATION UNDER 6 MONTHS

NO ACCOUNT TAKEN RE 'CONTINUOUS' BUT DO NOT COUNT TOWARDS 2/5-YEAR PERIOD

Provisions affecting the granting of decrees

Respondent could suffer

Grave financial

OR other hardship

caused by the granting of the decree

AND it would in all the circumstances be wrong to dissolve the marriage

All elements need to be satisfied

The application is made prior to the decree nisi and the court will consider all the circumstances of the case, including the conduct of the parties and their interests and those of any children or others.

Grave financial hardship

Usually arises through loss of pensions for older wives.

'Grave' – ordinary meaning – *Reiterbund v Reiterbund* (1975)

Subjective view taken re particular marriage but objective view taken of 'grave' – *Rukat v Rukat* (1975)

Hardship must be caused by the granting of the decree – *Talbot v Talbot* (1971)

Other payments may be made to compensate:

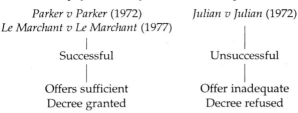

Parker v Parker (1972)   *Julian v Julian* (1972)
Le Marchant v Le Marchant (1977)

Successful   Unsuccessful

Offers sufficient   Offer inadequate
Decree granted   Decree refused

Wrong to dissolve the marriage

Even if the respondent can show 'grave financial or other hardship' it is also necessary to show that it would be wrong to dissolve the marriage. In *Brickell v Brickell* (1973) the respondent's wife was able to show grave financial hardship but because of her behaviour in spying on her husband and causing the failure of his business it was held that it would not be wrong to dissolve the marriage. The decree was granted.

This defence is available only in cases based on fact (s 1(2)(e)).

Section 10

In cases based on the facts in s 1(2)(d) and (e) then the respondent can apply to the court for considerations of his or her financial provision on divorce. This provision is contained in s 10(2) MCA 1973. Section 10(3) empowers the court not to make the decree absolute unless it is satisfied that the petitioner need not make any financial provision or that the provision made is reasonable and fair or the best that can be made in the circumstances.

In reaching its decision the court will consider all the circumstances, including the age, health, conduct, earning capacity and the financial resources and obligations of the parties.

Respondent can ask court, after decree nisi, to consider financial situation.

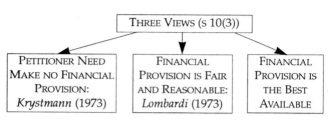

THREE VIEWS (s 10(3))		
PETITIONER NEED MAKE NO FINANCIAL PROVISION: *Krystmann* (1973)	FINANCIAL PROVISION IS FAIR AND REASONABLE: *Lombardi* (1973)	FINANCIAL PROVISION IS THE BEST AVAILABLE

Garcia (1992) – covers past and future provisions.

The court can delay the granting of the decree absolute if not satisfied.

The court can, however, still grant a decree if it is considered desirable to do so without delay, eg birth of a child imminent, s 10(4).

Under s 10(4) the court can make the decree absolute despite s 10(3) if the circumstances make it desirable to do so without delay or if it receives a satisfactory undertaking from the petitioner that he will make financial provisions for the respondent that the court may approve.

The undertaking must not be vague as the court must be able to enforce it. In the absence of specific proposals the court will decide on an appropriate order.

This provision only applies to divorces based on s 1(2)(d) and (e).

Section 41

This provision applies to all divorces where there are children involved. It does not depend on the application of the respondent. Under this provision, the court shall consider if there are any children of the family concerned and where there are such children, whether in the light of any proposed arrangements for the welfare of the children, it should exercise any of its powers under the Children Act 1989 in respect of any of them.

3 Ancillary relief

The welfare of minor children of the family (s 25(1))

The welfare of the children is not paramount under the MCA and will not override the other considerations. However, it is the first and most important consideration (*Suter v Suter and Jones* (1987)).

Financial resources (s 25(2)(a))

The court will consider all the financial resources of the parties, including those likely to arise in the future.

Financial obligations (s 25(2)(b))

To ensure a fair balance the court will also look to the future when considering on-going obligations.

Court looks at the reality of the situation: *Hardy v Hardy* (1981); *Newton v Newton* (1990)
The future must be considered – increase in earning capacity: *Mitchell v Mitchell* (1984)
Potential payer must have means to pay: *Brown v Brown* (1981)
New partner's income will only be considered as the effect of releasing more of the payer's resources for any orders to be made: *Macey v Macey* (1981)

Standard of living (s 25(2)(c))

The court's approach is to distribute any such reduction evenly without bringing either party below subsistence level.

Present and future obligations will be considered

The party keeping the children will have future obligations until they become independent: *Mesher v Mesher* (1980)

New families may need to be maintained as well as the former families. The court will attempt to balance the demands of both: *Stockford v Stockford* (1982)

When dealing with wealthy families it is often possible for the court to settle matters without any significant drop in living standards. The court will also consider the standard of living to which the parties have become accustomed and seek to maintain that standard.

Ages and duration of marriage (s 25(2)(d))

The ages of the parties can have an effect on the orders in as much as young couples are more likely to be involved in 'clean breaks' whilst older couples are more likely to make applications under ss 5 and 10 MCA 1973.

However, s 25A has always to be considered and if it is a short, childless marriage no order may be made or an order for a limited period only.

Cohabitation prior to marriage

> The courts will not normally equate marriage and cohabitation unless there is a significant degree of commitment: *Kokosinski v Kokosinski* (1980)

Physical or mental disability (s 25(2)(e))

> Allowances will be made for disability if it is possible to compensate by monetary means. If the disability deteriorates then allowances will be made: *Sakkas v Sakkas* (1987)

Contributions to the family welfare (s 25(2)(f))

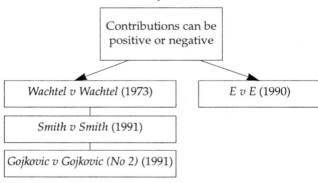

Contributions can be positive or negative

Wachtel v Wachtel (1973)

E v E (1990)

Smith v Smith (1991)

Gojkovic v Gojkovic (No 2) (1991)

Conduct it would be inequitable to disregard (s 25(2)(g))

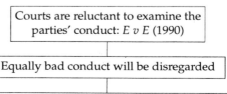

Courts are reluctant to examine the parties' conduct: *E v E* (1990)

Equally bad conduct will be disregarded

Will consider if 'both obvious and gross': *Kyte v Kyte* (1987)

Loss of future benefit (s 25(2)(h))

> Usually loss of pensions:
> *Parker v Parker* (1972)

Clean break provisions (s 25A)

The idea behind these provisions is to bring to an end any dependence or obligation between the parties as soon as is practicable depending on the circumstances of the case.

The court has a duty to consider a 'clean break' in each case (*Barrett v Barrett* (1988)). It does not have to apply the provisions. It will look at the situation in three ways:

> *Section 25A(1)*
> Is a 'clean break' appropriate?
>
> *Attar v Attar (No 2)* (1985)
> *Suter v Suter and Jones* (1987)
> *Scanlon v Scanlon* (1990)
> *Gojkovic v Gojkovic* (1990)

> *Section 25A(3)*
> If not, should it be dismissed and an order made preventing further application for periodical payments?
>
> *Seaton v Seaton* (1986)

> *Section 25A(2)*
> If so, can it be granted immediately or after a period of adjustment?
>
> *M v M* (1987)
> *Evans v Evans* (1990)

Sections 23, 24, 24A: Financial orders

> MCA 1973, s 23:
> Money orders

> Periodical payments
> Secured periodical payments
> Lump sums

> Periodical payments end on death of payer

> Secured periodical payments continue after the death of payer

> Both types end on the remarriage or death of the payee

> MCA 1973, s 24:
> Property orders

> Transfer of property
> Settlement of property
> Variation of a settlement
> Extinguish or reduce a settlement

> MCA 1973, s 24A

> Express power of sale

> All property in which either or both parties have an interest

> Available if court makes
> • secured periodical payments order
> • lump sum order
> • property adjustment order

Distribution of assets

There have been a number of guidelines laid down to provide assistance to the courts.

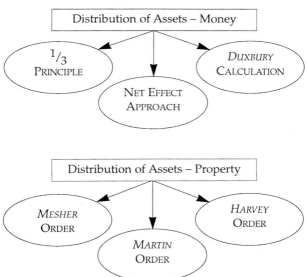

Property orders

The courts, in recent years, have also been more in favour of outright transfers of the property with only nominal payments of maintenance being ordered in return for the other spouse's loss of interest. This can suit a clean break situation. However, in a property slump, the order for the actual sale of a property may cause difficulties as it may not be sold for its proper value and so will raise insufficient funds to provide homes for both parties. These factors are of importance when considering the orders to be made.

Section 31 MCA: Variation of orders

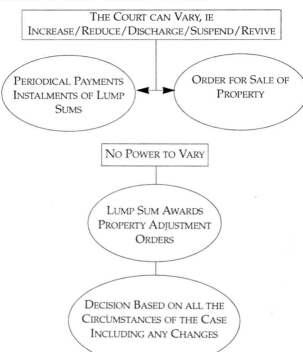

THE COURT CAN VARY, IE
INCREASE/REDUCE/DISCHARGE/SUSPEND/REVIVE

PERIODICAL PAYMENTS
INSTALMENTS OF LUMP
SUMS

ORDER FOR SALE OF
PROPERTY

NO POWER TO VARY

LUMP SUM AWARDS
PROPERTY ADJUSTMENT
ORDERS

DECISION BASED ON ALL THE
CIRCUMSTANCES OF THE CASE
INCLUDING ANY CHANGES

Also in common with s 25A, the 'clean break', the court has to consider whether to vary the order for a limited period under s 31(7). The court's attitude is similar to both situations, ie it is often reluctant to apply a clean break. The reluctance in the situation of variation usually shows itself when a party applies for the termination of an order. The court has to consider whether or not the payee would be able to adjust to the new circumstances without undue hardship, and a major factor in its judgment would be any future uncertainty. The approach of the courts is often to refuse to terminate the order but to reduce it to a nominal order so that if circumstances were to deteriorate for the payee then she could apply for a further variation and the existence of the nominal order could be seen as a safeguard.

It should be remembered that where the parties have agreed on the financial matters, and consent orders have been made, the limitations regarding lump sums, property adjustment orders still apply and if a variation of a consent order is sought then it will be necessary to show at least some of the following factors:

- fresh evidence coming to light which was not known at the time the order was made;

- the parties, including the court, relied on erroneous information;

- fraud or non-disclosure which would have led to a substantially different order;

- exceptionally, when the basis for the original order has been destroyed.

In order to avoid these hurdles, parties may appeal against an order out of time. However, there are strict limitations on this course of action and leave will only be granted if the applicant can meet the requirements laid down in the case of *Barder v Barder* (1987) which stated that only then would leave be granted.

The requirements are that:

- new events invalidate the basis of the order and an appeal would be likely to succeed;

- the new event occurred within a few months of the order;

- the application is made reasonably promptly; and

- the appeal, if granted, would not prejudice third parties who had acted in good faith and for valuable consideration on the basis of the order.

The main reason for such a strict approach is to prevent numerous applications and to maintain certainty in such situations.

Child Support Act 1991 (s 8(3))

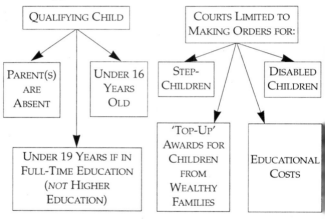

Welfare of the child is to be considered but is limited to the use of the formulae.

Child Support Agency

This body was set up by the Act to deal with the maintenance of children by absent parents. Applications will be made to the Agency by the parent with care for the child for an order against the absent parent and mathematical formulae are used by child support officers to fix any amount payable. Section 2 CSA 1991 states that the officers must have regard to the welfare of any child likely to be affected by decisions reached by their use of discretionary powers but since the major decisions are based on the formulae any discretion is limited.

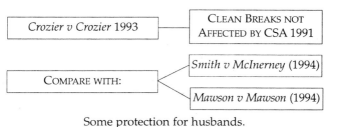

Some protection for husbands.

Child Support Act and clean breaks

Methods of assessment

These are dealt with only in outline due to their complexity. There is a set formula laid down in the Act and its attendant regulations for the assessment of the payment to be made by the absent parent. It is based on the income support payments in force at a particular time and is made up of the following elements:

- the child's maintenance requirements;

- assessable income of the parent with care AND the

absent parent;

- the maintenance assessment.

The child's maintenance requirement

This is made up of the income support payments that would be made to the child and the parent with care but with any child benefit payable deducted from the total.

Assessable incomes

The net income of each parent minus the element of the 'exempt income', ie the income support payment that would be payable or 50% of the income whichever is the greater, is calculated.

The maintenance assessment

The maintenance assessment is then reached by adding together the assessable incomes of both parents and multiplying the result by 0.5. The result will then determine the amount the absent parent has to contribute. If the result is less than or equal to the child's maintenance requirement then the absent parent will pay half his assessable income. If the result is more than the requirement then a further 25% of income becomes payable up to a maximum amount. This results in wealthier parents being made to pay proportionately more so that their child can benefit from their higher standard of living.

White Paper 1995: Improving Child Support

Introduced changes from April 1995:

- maximum 30% of absent parent's income payable as child support;

- allowances to be given for travel to work;

- allowances to take account of pre-1993 property transfers.

Further changes introduced in September and October 1995 by the Child Support Act 1995.

Introduced 'departures' from normal maintenance assessments.

'Departure orders' available for a number of grounds, eg extra costs arising from long-term illness/disability of applicant or dependant.

CSA 1995 has a phased implementation, some provisions coming into effect in 1996–97.

4 Property rights and disputes between spouses and cohabitees

Married Women's Property Act (MWPA) 1882 (s 17)

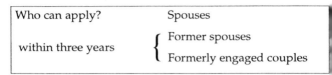

Who can apply?	Spouses
within three years	{ Former spouses { Formerly engaged couples

Unmarried couples cannot make use of s 17 but can ask the court to make a declaration of their rights. The decision will be reached on the same principles as s 17 cases.

How are s 17 MWPA decisions reached?

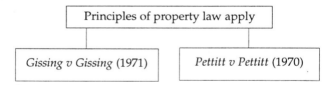

Principles of property law apply

Gissing v Gissing (1971)	*Pettitt v Pettitt* (1970)

Interests in land

Section 52 Law of Property Act (LPA) 1925 requires that all conveyances of land or any interest of land must be by way of deed. The conveyance can declare in whom the legal title is to vest and, in addition, may also declare in whom the beneficial title is to vest. The declaration made in the conveyance will be conclusive evidence of ownership in the absence of fraud or mistake (*Goodman v Gallant* (1986)).

The conveyance stated that the husband and wife were each entitled to half shares. The wife claimed a larger share but failed because of the express statements in the conveyance. However, the words used to make the declaration should be quite clear to avoid any difficulties in the future.

Resulting, implied or constructive trusts

Law of Property Act 1925, s 53(2) and Law of Property (Miscellaneous Provisions) Act 1989, s 2(5)

RESULTING, IMPLIED, CONSTRUCTIVE TRUSTS

- common intention that both parties have a beneficial interest in the property;

- non-legal owner acted to his or her detriment based on the common intention.

It can be said that a resulting trust arises from the actions of the parties and the courts give effect to their common intention or presumed common intention.

A constructive trust is said to arise from an operation of law whereby the court will imply a trust where it could be seen as almost permitting a fraud to allow one party to gain beneficial ownership considering how the parties have conducted themselves.

Direct financial contributions

Resulting trust
Where direct contributions are made and a beneficial interest is found, if there is no evidence to the contrary, then the shares will be decided in direct proportion to the contributions made by the parties (*Re Rogers Question* (1948)).

Although this is the normal situation, the court can vary the interests awarded if it finds sufficient evidence of intention (*Chapman v Chapman* (1969)).

Not all financial contributions will enable a non-owning party to claim a beneficial interest (*Savage v Dunningham* (1973)).

Constructive trust
It will be seen that a number of cases could have been dealt with as both resulting and constructive trusts. In these cases the parties claimed to have made contributions to the purchase of the property, albeit indirect rather than direct on the basis of a common intention as well as acting to their detriment.

The question of indirect contributions has caused difficulties over the years and it appears from Lord Bridge's judgment in *Lloyds Bank v Rosset* (1991) that such contributions are to be seen as doubtful as a basis for claiming any beneficial interests.

However, the nature and importance of these contributions have been considered in other, earlier cases to be of some importance and it is thought that the correct approach is that the judge should take a broad view of the situation and decide from it the parties' presumed intention as regards ownership. If the wife can show that her contributions towards the family finances released sufficient funds from the husband's resources to enable him to acquire the property then she may well succeed in her claim. Obviously, the more significant her contributions the greater her chances of success (*Grant v Edwards* (1986)).

Home improvements

Section 37 Matrimonial Proceedings and Property Act 1970
There are a number of requirements stated, each of which must be satisfied and use of the Act is restricted to married couples.

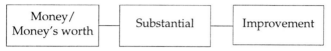

If these requirements are fulfilled and the court finds that there was an agreement that they led to an interest or an increased interest or, in the absence of an agreement, the court finds it just to grant an interest then the court can do so but is limited to assess such a share or increase by reference to the increase in the value of the property bought about by the improvement.

Although the court may infer an agreement if there is no express agreement, it will not normally do so unless it can be shown that the work done is of the type that would only be done if the party responsible for it were to acquire an interest in the property.

As already stated, this Act does not pertain to unmarried couples. However, they can rely on inferred intention arising from the nature of the work done being such as to gain the applicant an interest.

In *Cook v Head* (1972) the woman did much heavy labouring and demolition work, and along with the fact that both parties had saved towards the mortgage this was deemed sufficient for her to acquire an interest.

Proprietary estoppel

This concept can be seen as being similar to a constructive trust in as much as the person claiming an interest in the property must have acted to her detriment. Here, however, these actions are based on her being misled by the other party whereas under a constructive trust there must be acting to the detriment on the basis of a commence intention.

The recent Court of Appeal case of *Matharu v Matharu* (1994) provides us with a useful example of the factors considered in such circumstances.

The Court of Appeal held, by a majority, that the defendant had satisfied the necessary elements to establish proprietary estoppel. The Court quoted the case of *Wilmott v Barber* (1880) which had listed the requirements:

- that that person had made a mistake as to his or her legal rights;

- that she had expended some money or done some act on the faith of that mistaken belief;

- that the possessor of the legal right knew of the existence of the legal right which was inconsistent with the equity, if it existed;

- that the possessor of the legal right knew of the other person's mistaken belief;

- that the possessor of the legal right had encouraged the other person in the expenditure of money or in doing other acts on which that person relied.

Another case containing a useful definition of proprietary estoppel is *Re Basham* (1987). 'Where one person, A, has acted to his detriment on the faith of a belief, which was known to, and encouraged by, another person, B, that he either has been, or is going to, be given a right in, or over, B's property, B cannot insist on strict legal rights if to do so would be inconsistent with A's belief.'

Contractual licence

These situations may well arise in circumstances where a cohabitee is unable to show the requirements of a trust but can, at least, try to gain some protection by a contractual licence which will give her a right of occupation. If a contractual licence is shown to exist it will not give any proprietary rights but will allow the injured party to claim damages if that right is breached.

The requirements of a contractual licence are those found in other types of contract, ie an intention to be legally bound and consideration being supplied by the person seeking protection.

The situation is, to say the least, inconsistent and a closer look at the cases will show that trying to predict the outcome of a case will be difficult (cf *Tanner v Tanner* (1975) and *Horrocks v Forray* (1976)).

Sharing the spoils: equitable accounting

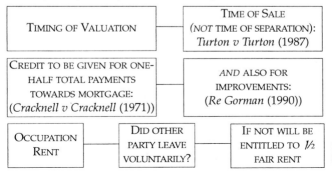

LPA 1925 s 30

As often happens on the breakdown of a relationship, be it marriage or cohabitation, one of the parties may want to remain in the property whilst the other will want to sell to realise his assets.

Under this section the court has the power to 'make such orders as it thinks fit'. This does not mean that the court can alter the parties' interests but it can decide whether or not to order the sale.

The decision is based on whether or not the purpose for the purchase of the property is still in existence. If it still exists then neither party can insist on the sale; if it has come to an end then the duty to sell prevails.

Protection against third parties

Such protection against third parties is often essential for spouses or partners in situations where the other partner has incurred liabilities which he has failed to meet and the loss of the family home could result. The usual situation is where the home has been used to secure a mortgage. (*Williams and Glyn's Bank v Boland* (1980); *Kingsnorth Finance v Tizard* (1986)).

Rights of occupation

It must be remembered that a right of occupation will not create or increase any proprietary interest a party may have in the matrimonial home, as was seen in the cases concerning contractual licences. However, rights of occupation provide an important form of protection in a number of difficult situations.

The main source of such protection for spouses is the Matrimonial Homes Act 1983.

s 1(1)	NON-ENTITLED SPOUSE
s 1(11)	SPOUSE WITH EQUITABLE INTEREST
s 9	JOINT OWNERS

Rights:

- if in occupation, a right not to be evicted or excluded from the dwelling house or any part thereof, by the other spouse except with the leave of the court given by a court under this section.

- if not in occupation, a right with the leave of the court so given to enter into and occupy the dwelling house.

Basically, those in the home cannot be evicted or excluded, those not in occupation can enter and occupy the home.

Registration

Registered Land:	Notice under LRA 1925
Unregistered Land:	Class F Land Charge, Land Charges Act 1972

Another way in which the protection can be lost after registration is when the spouse abuses the registration, as in *Wroth v Tyler* (1973).

The property need not be owned by the spouses as the Act also covers rented housing, be it in the public or private sector, as long as the requirements of s 1(1) are met, eg only one spouse has a legal agreement to occupy. This could in some circumstances weaken the wife's position. If the husband breached his contract, eg by failing to pay the rent, he may lose his right to occupy the property and if he does so then neither party has a right of occupation.

Payments to assist occupying spouse

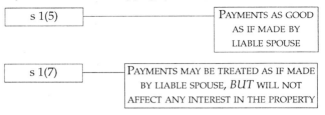

This amounts to the wife being able to reside in the house by paying the mortgage and preventing the building society from repossessing it whilst not gaining a beneficial interest in the property.

Also under s 36 Administration of Justice Act 1970, if the mortgage is in joint names and one spouse fails to make the payments, then the other can apply for the proceedings to be delayed if it appears to the court that the other spouse can make the payments due within a reasonable time.

Following *Richards v Richards* (1984), decisions regarding occupation of the family home will be based on the considerations contained in s 1(3) MHA. The relevance of the considerations will become apparent during the following chapter on domestic violence, when the majority of cases dealing with rights of occupation occur.

If orders are made by the court, s 5 MHA states that the orders end on the death of either party or on termination of the marriage unless, under the power in s 2, the court has directed otherwise during the marriage.

5 Domestic violence

Matrimonial Homes Act 1983

The orders available under s 1 MHA have already been dealt with under the section dealing with a spouse's rights of occupation of the family home and this is generally a major part of the protection being sought in domestic violence situations.

Either spouse may apply for an order:

- declaring, enforcing, restricting, or terminating rights;

- prohibiting, suspending or restricting the exercise by either spouse of the right to occupy the dwelling house; or

- requiring either spouse to permit the exercise by the other of that right.

Applicants for MHA orders

Who can Apply?	Married couples only

Statutory Criteria:	s 1(3) MHA *Richards* (1984) 'just and reasonable'

Considerations include:

- the conduct of the spouses towards each other and others;

- their financial needs and resources;

- the needs of any children;

- all the circumstances of the case.

Conduct

The question will obviously arise as to whether or not a spouse has actually used physical violence against the other. If there is no evidence of violence then it could be difficult to obtain an ouster order.

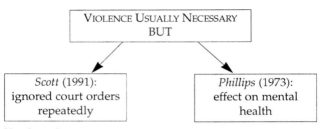

Needs and resources

The most important issue that arises in this area is that of accommodation for the parties. The court will have to consider how easy it will be for the respective spouses to be able to find new accommodation. If the wife has everyday care of the children then she would obviously find it more difficult to find alternative housing than the husband, who would find it relatively easy, especially in the private sector.

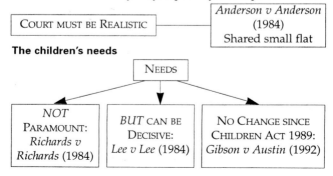

An important point to bear in mind when considering the needs of the children is the Children Act 1989. Section 8(4) of the Children Act contains the measures deemed to be 'family proceedings' and amongst those mentioned are the Matrimonial Homes Act 1983, the Domestic Violence and Matrimonial Homes Act 1976 and the Domestic Proceedings and Magistrates' Court Act 1978. When dealing with matters under these Acts regarding the occupation of the family home the court may, but is not obliged to, consider making s 8 orders with respect to the child, but when dealing with the ouster or exclusion element of the application the Children Act has not affected the decision in *Richards* in as much as their needs are not to be seen as paramount.

Other circumstances of the case

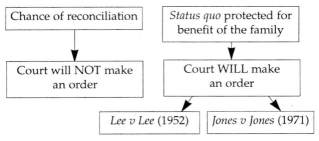

The Matrimonial Homes Act contains the statutory criteria for decisions in this area but also contains weaknesses. These are that the Act can only be used by married couples, there is no power of arrest available nor is there an ability to make a non-molestation order. These weaknesses can be avoided by making a joint application under the Matrimonial Homes Act and the Domestic Violence and Matrimonial Proceedings Act 1976.

Domestic Violence and Matrimonial Proceedings Act 1976

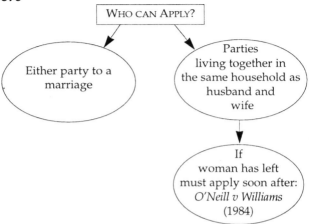

Also, if the couple indicate that they will continue to live together as in the case of *F v F* (1989) then the court will not usually grant the application as the Act is not seen as being intended to be used as a way of controlling the parties' behaviour towards each other, especially by the threat of court action.

Under s 1(1) of the Act the court can grant an injunction containing one or more of the following provisions:

- restraining the other party from molesting the applicant;

- restraining the other party from molesting a child living with the applicant;

- excluding the other party from any part of the matrimonial home or from a specified area in which the matrimonial home is included;

- requiring the other party to permit the applicant to enter and remain in the matrimonial home.

Children who can be protected

NB: Child living with the applicant

It must be remembered that decisions on applications made under DVMPA must be based on the same considerations as those made under the MHA (ie those contained in s 1(3) MHA) and due thought is given to the draconian nature of the order.

Definition of molestation

| Molestation: very wide definition | *F v F* (1989) *Johnson v Walton* (1990) |

An area of advantage for the applicant using the DVMPA is that the respondent can be excluded from an area around the family home but this must be within reason to fit the circumstances of the case and would not usually cover the applicant's place of work but may if it is close to her home.

These injunctions are seen in most cases as a short-term remedy and as such are only needed for a limited period.

Duration of orders

| Time limit | Usually three months but can be indefinite: *Galan v Galan* (1985) |

Another advantage of the DVMPA is that there is a power of arrest that can be attached to the injunction if the requirements of s 2 are met.

Where an order has been made restraining the other party from using violence against the applicant or the child or excluding the other part from the matrimonial home or from a specified area in which the home is included then the judge may attach a power of arrest to the injunction if he is satisfied that:

- the other party has caused actual bodily harm to the applicant or to the child; and

- considers that he is likely to do so again.

Level of violence

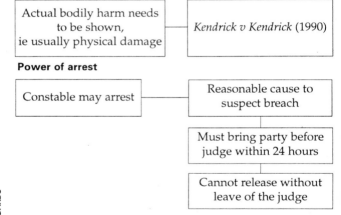

Actual bodily harm needs to be shown, ie usually physical damage	*Kendrick v Kendrick* (1990)

Power of arrest

Constable may arrest	Reasonable cause to suspect breach

Must bring party before judge within 24 hours

Cannot release without leave of the judge

Power of arrest must be registered at the local police station to the applicant's address.

Time limit: usually three months.

Under the DVMPA the court has the power to grant a non-molestation and/or exclusion order in an *ex parte* application and has the ability to attach a power of arrest but the use of the power is extremely rare. It must be shown that there is 'real immediate danger of serious injury or incurable damage' before the court will grant an interim order on an *ex parte* application (*Practice Note (Matrimonial Causes: Injunction: ex parte Applications) 1978*) and if the other party is readily available for service then it is unlikely to be made. If any form of order is made then it will be strictly limited in time.

Domestic Proceedings and Magistrates' Court Act 1978

Who can apply?	Married couples only

Section 16(2) allows the court, where satisfied that the respondent has used or threatened to use violence against the person of the applicant or a child of the family and that it is necessary for the protection of the applicant or a child of the family that an order should be made under this subsection, to make one or both of the following orders:

- that the respondent shall not use or threaten to use violence against the person of the applicant;

- that the respondent shall not use or threaten to use violence against the person of a child of the family.

Section 16(3) says that where an application is made under this subsection and the court is satisfied that the respondent has used violence against the applicant or a child of the family; or the respondent has threatened to use violence against the person of the applicant or a child of the family and has used violence against some third person; or that the respondent has in contravention of an order made under subsection (2) threatened to use violence against the person of the applicant or the person of a child of the family, and that the applicant or a child of the family is in danger of being physically injured by the respondent (or would be in such danger if the applicant or child were to enter the matrimonial home) the court may make one or both of the following orders:

- an order requiring the respondent to leave the matrimonial home;

- an order prohibiting the respondent from entering the matrimonial home.

Factors to consider in DVMPA cases

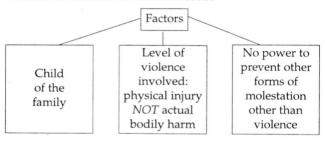

Power of arrest

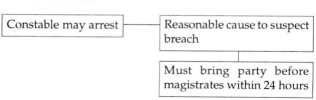

Magistrates must give reasons for the decision to attach the power of arrest: *Widdowson v Widdowson* (1982).

The inherent jurisdiction of the court

If other proceedings are pending between the parties then the High Court and the county court can in certain circumstances grant an injunction to protect the woman. However, this must be in support of an existing legal or equitable right *Ainsbury v Millington* (1986). Also there must be a lack of statutory power covering the situation to enable the court to use this jurisdiction.

In this case the parties who were unmarried were joint tenants of a council flat. After a period of separation the woman married another man and tried to exclude the man from the property.

She was unable to make an application under the MHA since they were unmarried and she was unable to use the DPMCA as they were no longer living together as man and wife in the same household. She made an application under the Supreme Court Act 1981 but the application failed on a number of grounds including the fact that the woman did not have the sole right and so no greater right to occupy the property than the man, and the court will not grant an order where it will merely give one party an advantage over the other in domestic proceedings. It was also deemed to be unnecessary to grant an order to protect the children of the relationship.

Undertakings

To remove the need for a full hearing and the calling of evidence the party that would otherwise be the subject of the application can agree to give to the court an undertaking that he will not molest the other party and/or will leave the family home as would have been requested by the other party depending on the circumstances of the case.

When such an undertaking is given it will be as binding on the party giving it as if an order had been made by the court (*Hussain v Hussain* (1986)).

6 Children I

An important case that illustrates the change in attitude towards parents and their relationship with their children is *Gillick v West Norfolk and Wisbech AHA* (1986).

This case brought into being the concept of the 'Gillick competent' child which will be seen as an important development which has been enlarged by the Children Act 1989.

The Family Law Reform Act 1969 had given young people over the age of 16 the statutory right to consent to medical treatment but there was no legal guidance as to the extent of parental rights over children under 16 who required medical advice as was the case in *Gillick*. In any case, regarding the extent of parental rights, matters had to be decided in the light of what was best for the child and this could vary with the child's age and understanding and that a child with sufficient maturity could be allowed to make his own decisions, although it will be seen later in this chapter that even though this is now generally accepted there will be times when the court will still overrule children normally seen as 'Gillick competent' in exceptional circumstances (usually medical cases).

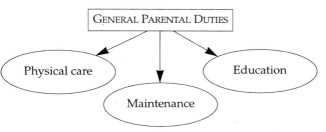

The latest attitude towards what is expected of parents is shown by the concept of parental responsibility contained in the Children Act 1989.

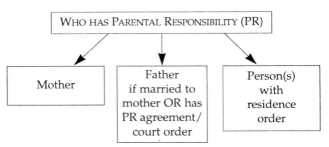

Person(s) with PR can act independently of others except:
- if consent required from all with PR;
- in contravention of court order.

Parental responsibility cannot be given away. The parents will retain it even if they divorce, if the child is made the subject of a care order they will share it with the local authority, and they cannot transfer it to another party in an attempt to avoid their responsibilities. Parental responsibility can be brought to an end by the child being adopted resulting in the parental responsibility being vested in the adoptive parents on the child reaching maturity, marrying or joining the armed forces.

Children Act 1989

The Children Act 1989 came into effect on 14 October 1991 and introduces a new philosophy of non-intervention by the state in the affairs of the family unless it is deemed necessary to protect the children from suffering significant harm and even if any action is deemed necessary then if possible the action should be taken whilst the child remains within the family. An important aim of the Act is to provide a flexible, consistent set of remedies and orders which would be available at all levels of the legal system and to make them available, whether the matter be one of private or public law. This attempt at unification of both areas of law has been largely successful and has provided much of the sought-after flexibility.

Welfare and delay principles

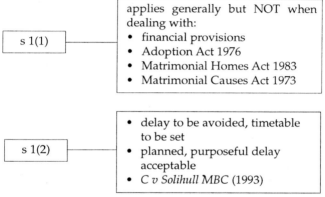

| s 1(1) | applies generally but NOT when dealing with:
• financial provisions
• Adoption Act 1976
• Matrimonial Homes Act 1983
• Matrimonial Causes Act 1973 |

| s 1(2) | • delay to be avoided, timetable to be set
• planned, purposeful delay acceptable
• *C v Solihull MBC* (1993) |

Section 1(3) contains what has become commonly known as the 'checklist' and contains the factors that the court is required to consider when dealing with the circumstances mentioned in s 1(4), ie:

• the court is considering whether to make vary or discharge a s 8 order and the making, variation or discharge of the order is opposed by any party to the proceedings; or

• the court is considering whether to make, vary or discharge an order under Part IV.

Note the fact that there will be opposition to the application. The factors to be considered are:

- the ascertainable wishes and feeling of the child concerned (considered in the light of his age and understanding);
- his physical, emotional and educational needs;
- the likely effect on him of any change in his circumstances;
- his age, sex, background and any characteristic of his which the court considers relevant;
- any harm which he has suffered or is at risk of suffering;
- how capable each of his parents and any other person in relation to whom the court considers the question to be relevant is of meeting his needs;
- the range of powers available to the court under the Act in the proceedings in question.

Section 1(5) illustrates the basis of the philosophy underlying the Act. This is one of the most influential principles contained in the Act, ie the principle of non-intervention by the state in the family. It provides:

> ... where a court is considering whether or not to make one or more orders under this Act with respect to a child, it shall not make that order or any of the orders unless it considers that doing so would be better for the child than making no order at all.

The new orders

An important aim of the Act was to introduce a new range of orders which would provide courts at all levels with a flexibility to enable them to deal with matters occurring across the spectrum of family law matters, be they private or public law matters. These new orders are contained in s 8 of

Part II of the Act and, not surprisingly, have become known collectively as 'section 8 orders'.

The orders are:

- residence orders;
- contact orders;
- prohibited steps orders;
- specific issues orders.

Section 10(1) of the Act gives the court the power to make s 8 orders in any family proceedings in which a question arises with respect to the welfare of any child if:

- an application for the order has been made by a person who:

  (a) is entitled to apply for a s 8 order with respect to the child; or

  (b) has obtained the leave of the court to make the application; or

- the court considers that the order should be made even though no such application has been made.

The first point of note is 'What are family proceedings?' The definition is contained in s 8(3) and (4).

Section 8(3)

For the purposes of this Act 'family proceedings' means any proceedings:

(a) under the inherent jurisdiction of the High Court in relation to children; and

(b) under the enactments mentioned in subsection (4), but does not include proceedings on an application for leave under s 100(3).

Section 8(4)

The enactments are:

(a) Parts I, II, and IV of this Act;
(b) the Matrimonial Causes Act 1973;
(c) the Domestic Violence and Matrimonial Proceedings Act 1976;
(d) the Adoption Act 1976;
(e) the Domestic Proceedings and Magistrates' Courts Act 1978;
(f) ss 1 and 9 of the Matrimonial Homes Act 1983;
(g) Part III of the Matrimonial and Family Proceedings Act 1984.

Residence orders

Residence orders settle the arrangements to be made as to the person with whom the child is to live.

A residence order most frequently occurs in family breakdown situations and is used to settle disputes over what was previously known as custody. The intention behind the order is not just to decide who has possession of the child: it will also mean they take on the everyday responsibilities of care for the child. Because of this, the matter of parental responsibility must be considered because to fulfil this task the person with the residence order must be able to take everyday decisions regarding the upbringing of the child. If it is granted to a married parent then it will not alter the situation that each parent will retain parental responsibility and each is able to act independently for the benefit of the child. If the order is granted to an unmarried father then the court is obliged to grant him parental responsibility by way of a s 4 'parental responsibility order' (s 12(1)) and he will share it with the mother.

If the order is granted to a non-parent then they will be granted parental responsibility (s 12(2)) which they will share with the parent, but it will be limited in as much as the non-parent will be unable to consent to or refuse to consent to an adoption or appoint a guardian (s 12(3)).

Limits on residence orders

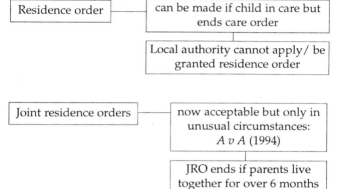

Following the granting of a residence order the contents of s 13 of the Act must be considered. It states that if such an order is in force then no person may:

- cause the child to be known by a new surname; or
- remove him from the UK for over one month;

without the written consent of every person who has parental responsibility for the child or the leave of the court.

The court will reach its decision on the matter of a change of surname by following the principles laid down in *W v A (Child: Surname)* (1981).

Again, when considering whether to grant leave for the child to leave the country, the court must bear in mind the contents of s 1, ie the welfare principle, the checklist and the 'no order' principle. The cases which occur in this area often concern a family wishing to emigrate with the child.

Contact orders

This an order requiring the person with whom the child lives or is to live to allow the child to visit or to stay with the person named in the order or for that and the child otherwise to have contact with each other.

The order covers the area formerly known as access. It allows the non-resident parent or any other person named in the order to retain contact with the child in a way to be decided by the court. This could be by stays, visits, letters or telephone calls, depending on the circumstances of the case.

Courts attitude to contact

$M \, v \, M$ (1973)	contact with parents is the right of the child, *NOT* of the parents

When reaching its decision on the matter of contact, the court must bear in mind that the paramount consideration is the welfare of the child and if there is conflict between the parties then the s 1(3) checklist must also be borne in mind. This is frequently the case as these orders are usually sought in cases of family breakdown and bitterness and resentment can lead to a failure to reach an amicable agreement.

The accepted approach to the subject of contact is that there is a presumption that the child will benefit by retaining contact with both parents and contact should be allowed unless it can be shown to be detrimental to the child's welfare, as was illustrated in *Re H (Minors) (Access)* (1992). If there is a contested application for contact then it is a matter for the court to decide on s 1 considerations.

Under usual circumstances it will be seen that a contact order will be granted to allow contact between the child and a non-resident parent, but the problem has arisen of whether a contact order can be made ordering that there be no contact between them. Although there is still some discussion as to whether it is the correct approach to the problem, in the case of *Nottinghamshire County Council v P (No 2)* (1993) it was held that such an order could be made.

Section 11(7) allows the court to attach directions as to how s 8 orders are to be carried out and can attach conditions.

This power can be used in cases where, for example, contact is seen as being in the child's interests, but there may be a need for such contact to be supervised.

Supervised contact

| IF CONTACT NEEDS TO BE SUPERVISED |
| eg sexual abuse cases where contact to continue |

| CORRECT METHOD VIA S 16 FAMILY ASSISTANCE ORDER |
| *Re DH (A Minor) (Child Abuse)* (1994) |

Residence orders and contact orders are considered to be the primary orders contained in s 8 of the Act. Prohibited steps orders and specific issues orders are seen as secondary orders, as is illustrated by the restrictions placed on their use by s 9(5).

Because of this subsection the court cannot exercise its power to make either order with a view to achieving a result which could be achieved by making a residence order or a contact order or in any way which is denied to the High Court (by s 100(2)) in the exercise of its inherent jurisdiction with respect to children. It is said that it prevents the use of such orders to gain certain aims via 'the back door' approach and ensures that the primary orders and inherent jurisdiction are used in the appropriate circumstances.

In *Nottinghamshire County Council v P* (1993) it was held that a prohibited steps order which prevented contact between the father and the children and excluded him from the family home could not be allowed to stand as it was seen as achieving a result which could be achieved by the making of a residence order or a contact order, and the local authority was attempting to use the 'back door' approach to the problem.

Prohibited steps orders

These are defined in the Act as 'an order that no step which could be taken by a parent in meeting his parental responsibility for a child and which is of the kind specified in the order shall be taken by any person without the consent of the court'.

It will be seen that the order covers steps which fall within the area of parental responsibility and so is to some extent limited in its application in as much as it cannot to be used to prevent steps which would not come within this ambit, eg assault or molestation and other measures would be needed in those circumstances.

This type of order is meant to deal with individual or single issues in a particular case and is meant to prevent a particular step being taken. A common example would be an order preventing the removal of a child from the UK in a case where there was no residence order in force and so no prohibition under s 13 to prevent such removal.

Normally such an order would be made against one of the parents of the child who can, as we have seen, exercise his responsibility alone, provided it is not incompatible with a court order. However, this order can be made against 'any person'. A person who could be named in the order could be any person that could take a step which could be taken via parental responsibility. This could include a teacher or an unmarried father who does not have parental responsibility and could be prevented from consenting to medical treatment for the child.

Specific issues orders

This is defined as:

> an order giving a direction for the purpose of determining a specific question which has arisen or which may arise in connection with any aspect of parental responsibility for a child.

Again, it will be seen that it is to deal with normally a single issue and so is similar to a prohibited steps order and is also limited by the matter being within the area of parental responsibility. Where there is a dispute between the parents on a specific matter the court can resolve the matter by granting this type of order and stating the necessary course of action. Such an area of conflict could be the issue of a child's education as was the case in *Re P (A Minor) (Education)* (1992).

Another important case involving the granting of a specific issues order was *Re HG (Specific Issue: Procedure)* (1993) where it was held that as there was an element of parental responsibility present in deciding the question of the child's treatment then the availability of a specific issue order was beyond question. The procedure for deciding such questions was also laid down for use in future cases.

Who can apply for s 8 orders ?

Section 10(4)
The following persons are entitled to apply to the court for any s 8 order with respect to a child:

(a) any parent or guardian of the child;

(b) any person in whose favour a residence order is in force with respect to the child.

Section 10(5)
The following persons are entitled to apply for a residence or contact order with respect to the child:

(a) any party to a marriage (whether or not subsisting) in relation to whom the child is a child of the family;

(b) any person with whom the child has lived for a period of at least three years;

(c) any person who:

(i) in any case where a residence order is in force with respect to the child has the consent of each of the persons in whose favour the order was made;

(ii) in any case where the child is in the care of the local authority has the consent of that authority;

(iii) in any other case has the consent of each of those (if any) who have parental responsibility for the child.

An example of the flexibility brought into the area of remedies available under the Children Act is that fact that any person can apply for a s 8 order. If they are not included in the above groups then they must apply to the court for leave to apply for an order (s 10(a)(ii)).

The factors the court has to consider when dealing with an application for leave are contained in s 10(9):

(a) the nature of the proposed application for the s 8 order;

(b) the applicant's connection with the child;

(c) any risk there might be of that proposed application disrupting the child's life to such an extent that he would be harmed by it; and

(d) where the child is being looked after by a local authority –

    (i) the authority's plans for the child's future and the wishes and feelings of the child's parents.

Welfare principle in leave applications

A problem which could arise in cases where the child has been in foster care is contained in s 9(3). Where the child is, or has been, at any time within the last six months, in foster care then the person who had care of the child, ie the foster parent, may not apply for leave to apply for a s 8 order unless:

- he has the consent of the authority;
- he is a relative of the child; or
- the child has lived with him for at least three years preceding the application.

The time period mentioned in this restriction need not be continuous but must have begun not more than five years before the making of the application.

When can children apply for s 8 orders?

A child needing advice may well be able to help himself by applying for a s 8 order.

He must apply for leave to apply for such an order and the court in order to grant leave must be satisfied that the child has sufficient understanding to make the proposed application. This will obviously be judged on the age and maturity of the particular child involved in each case and because of the difficulties which arise in such cases such applications should be heard by the High Court (*Practice Direction* (1993)).

Child applications for leave

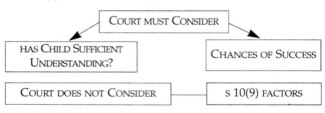

Family assistance order

A new type of order introduced by the Children Act is the Family Assistance order contained in s 16 of the Act.

In family proceedings the court can make a family assistance order requiring either a probation officer or a local authority officer, usually a social worker, to be made available to advise, assist and befriend any person named in the order. However, before the order can be made the local authority must agree to making the officer available (s 16(7)).

The persons that can be named in the order are those mentioned in s 16(2). They are:

- the child himself;

- the parent or guardian of the child;

- any person with whom the child is living or who has a contact order in his favour in respect of the child.

These persons, with the exception of the child, who are named in the order are also required to consent to the order being made (s 16(3)). The order can only be made for a maximum of six months and will only be available in exceptional circumstances.

This order will only be made by the court on its own motion and no applications can be made for this type of order.

Private law

Family breakdown, s 1(3)

In the event of a family breakdown the court will consider the following when ensuring satisfactory arrangements for the children involved:

- the ascertainable wishes and feelings of the child concerned (considered in the light of his age and understanding);

- his physical emotional and educational needs;

- the likely effect on him of any change in his circumstances;

- his age, sex, background and any other characteristics of his which the court considers relevant;

- any harm which he has suffered or is at risk of suffering;

- how capable each of his parents and any other person in relation to whom the court considers the question to be relevant is of meeting his needs;

- the range of powers available to the court under this Act in the proceedings in question.

The ascertainable wishes and feelings of the child

This factor develops the philosophy of '*Gillick*' competence and the child's wishes will be judged in the light of his age and understanding.

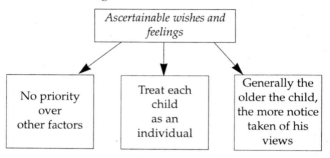

The child's physical, emotional and educational needs

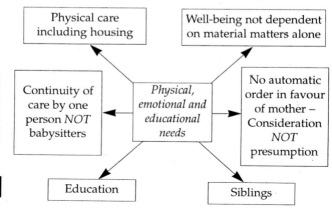

The likely effect on the child of any change in his or her circumstances

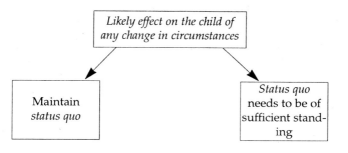

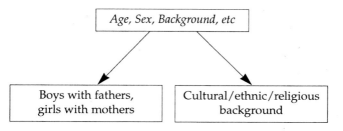

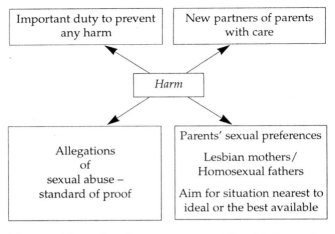

The capability of each parent to meet the child's needs

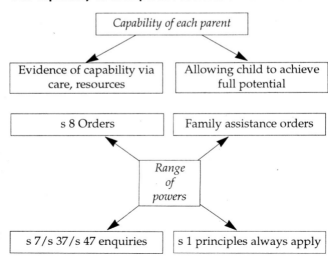

Financial provision and property adjustment for children

Section 15 and Schedule 1 of the Children Act 1989 set out the provisions for financial relief for children. An application for financial relief comes within the definition of 'family proceedings' and a court hearing such an application may also make s 8 orders. The orders the court can make are orders for periodical payments, lump sums, settlements and transfers of property. However, if the application is made in the family proceedings court then only the monetary orders are available, not the property orders.

Guardianship

The position is now much more restricted than prior to the implementation of the Children Act, and the only methods of making an appointment are contained in s 5 of the Act.

Section 5(1) gives the court the power to appoint an individual who applies to be a guardian in respect of a child if:

- the child has no parent with parental responsibility for him; or

- a residence order has been made in respect of the child in favour of a parent or guardian who has died while the order was in force.

The revocation and disclaimer of an appointment

Section 6 says that a later appointment by a parent or guardian will be taken to revoke the earlier appointment unless it is clear (either by express provision or necessary implication) that the purpose of the later appointment is to make an additional appointment.

It also allows the parent to revoke the appointment by another written document which meets the requirements needed for an appointment or by destroying the original document. If the appointment is made by will then this must be revoked.

If a person has been appointed as a child's guardian but wishes to disclaim his appointment then he can do so by an instrument in writing signed by him which must be made within a reasonable time of his first knowing that the appointment has taken effect. The obvious way to avoid difficulties would be to consult with the person to be appointed prior to making the arrangements thus making a disclaimer unnecessary.

The court has the power to bring an appointment of a guardian to an end on the application of any person with parental responsibility, on the application of the child concerned with leave of the court and in any family proceedings if the court considers it should be brought to an end even though no application has been made.

The court when dealing with matters of guardianship should apply the principles contained in s 1(1)(2) and (5) and although it need not apply the checklist in s 1(3), it will normally do so.

7   Children II

Care and supervision orders

Since the Children Act 1989 came into effect there is now only one way that a child can be placed into the care of a local authority or be made subject to a supervision order, and that is by the applicant being able to satisfy the requirements of s 31(2) of the Act and showing that the welfare of the child demands that the order be made. Wardship can no longer be used to make a child the subject of these orders.

Most care proceedings will commence in the family proceedings court but matters may be transferred to a county court or the High Court if it is considered appropriate since all these courts have jurisdiction to deal with care matters as they fall within the definition of 'family proceedings'.

Who can apply for a care or supervision order?

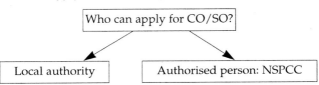

If the court is dealing with matters which are considered to be 'family proceedings' and it considers that a local authority should investigate the circumstances of the case it has the power to direct that the authority should do so (s 37(1)).

However, if the authority carries out the investigation but decides that an application for a care order is not, in its opinion, necessary, then the court cannot require the authority to make an application and this could mean that situations may arise when children may be left without measures being available to safeguard their welfare as occurred in the case of *Nottinghamshire County Council v P* (1993).

A care order or supervision order can only be made in respect of a child who is under 17 years of age (or 16 if the child is married).

The threshold criteria

When the local authority has decided that an application is to be made then it must be able to fulfil the requirements of s 31(2) which have become known as the 'threshold criteria'.

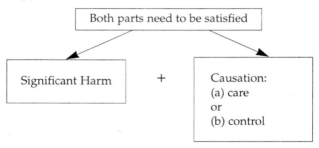

A vital element to remember is that even when the authority has been able to satisfy the 'threshold criteria', the court will be required to consider the contents of s 1 of the Act.

The welfare principle, delay principle and the 'no order' principle must be borne in mind before the final decision is made. They form the basis of the court's decision in all 'family proceedings'.

Section 31(9) contains the definitions of the terms used in the 'threshold criteria'.

'Harm'	ill-treatment or the impairment of health and development.
'Development'	physical, intellectual, emotional, social or behavioural development.
'Health'	physical or mental health.
'Ill-treatment'	includes sexual abuse and other forms of ill-treatment which are not physical.

Other definitions

| 'Significant' | Considerable, noteworthy, or important: *Humberside CC v B* (1993) |
| 'Care' | Normal physical and emotional care that a reasonable parent would give |

Test to apply to s 31(10)

When looking at the effect of any failings on the child, s 31(10) states that the child in question must be judged against what can be expected of a similar child having taken into account the characteristics of that child, ie take a subjective view of the child in question and apply an objective test when comparing him with a similar child.

The House of Lords decision in *Re M (A Minor) (Care Order: Threshold Conditions)* (1994) has settled that the time when judgment has to be made about significant harm being suffered is when the local authority commences proceedings for the protection of the child. This means the time the local authority takes any temporary measure which may lead to a care order application being made in the future.

The question of future harm which the child is 'likely to suffer' should be judged 'on the balance of probabilities'.

> *Re H and R (Child Sexual Abuse)* (1995)

The court should look at all the evidence and decide whether or not he will suffer harm in the future if no order is made. It has been held that the words should not be construed restrictively and a care order should be granted if indicated by the evidence (*Re A (A Minor) (Care Proceedings)* (1993)).

When looking at the second part of the criteria, the harm being considered must arise from the care being given by the child's parent not being what would be expected from a reasonable parent, ie an objective test.

However, when looking at the element of being 'beyond parental control' it need not be the parent's fault. It may be that if the parent has tried to discipline the child but has failed, the child would then be beyond control and could be the subject of an application. The parent could ask the local authority to make such an application but it will be up to the authority to decide whether or not to do so.

How decisions on care orders will be reached

s 31(2) minimum requirement
Then court will consider s 1 factors to decide if care order to be made

The effects of a care order

While a care order (CO) is in force in respect of the child the local authority will have parental responsibility for him (s 33).

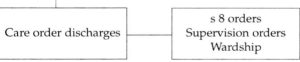

| Local authority gets parental responsibility | shares with parents but local authority senior partner |

Can limit parents' use of parental responsibility *ONLY* if necessary for child's welfare

Other restrictions on local authority – may not:

(a) change the child's religion;
(b) change the child's name;
(c) agree or refuse to agree to the child's adoption;
(d) consent or refuse to the making of a freeing order;
(e) change the child's surname or remove him from the UK without the written consent of every person with parental responsibility for the child or the leave of the court.

| Care order discharges | s 8 orders
Supervision orders
Wardship |

It is important to remember that the court will not interfere with the way the local authority will implement a care order. Since it is seen that Parliament intended that local authorities should be trusted to do as they see fit when dealing with children in their care and the court, having had the opportunity to study the authority's plan when deciding to make the order, should allow the authority to manage the situation and should not attach conditions to a care order (*Re T (A Minor) (Care Order: Conditions)* (1994)).

Parental contact with a child in care

Section 34 of the Act states that there is a statutory presumption that the authority must allow the child to have reasonable contact with groups of people after the granting of the order and the authority is expected to present its proposals for contact in its plans put before the court.

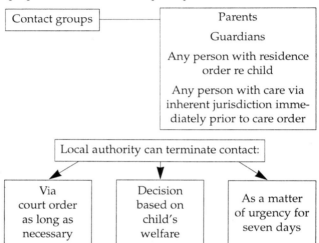

Contact groups	Parents
	Guardians
	Any person with residence order re child
	Any person with care via inherent jurisdiction immediately prior to care order

Local authority can terminate contact:

Via court order as long as necessary	Decision based on child's welfare	As a matter of urgency for seven days

The effects of a supervision order

When an application has been made under s 31(1), the court has the power to grant either a care order or a supervision order if the authority has fulfilled the 'threshold criteria'.

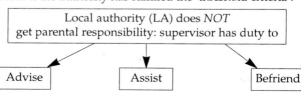

Local authority (LA) does *NOT* get parental responsibility: supervisor has duty to

Advise	Assist	Befriend

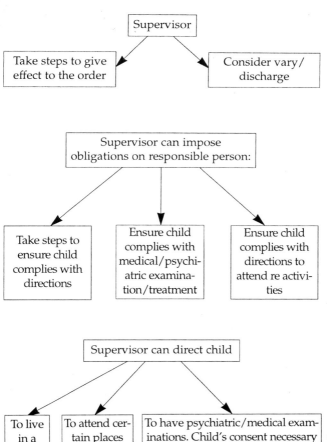

Duration: one year – possible extension up to three years.

Interim care and supervision orders

In certain circumstances, the court will be unable to reach a conclusion as to how to finally deal with a case and may need to make an interim order until further enquiries have been made and reports submitted for its consideration.

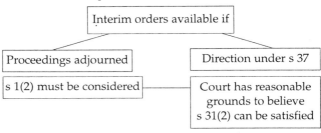

Duration: maximum eight weeks; no limit on number made.

Discharge of a care order

The court will decide the matter on the principles contained in s 1 of the Act.

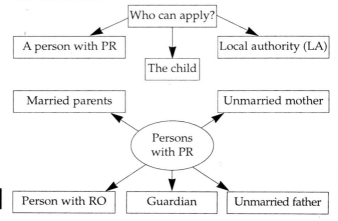

Others would need leave to apply for RO. If granted RO would vest PR in applicant and end CO. If applicant LA, court may substitute CO by SO – no need to prove s 31(2) again. If application refused, no further applications within six months without leave of court.

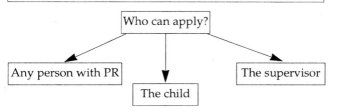

Appointment of a guardian *ad litem*

Section 41(1) of the Act states that in care and supervision proceedings a guardian *ad litem* (GAL) must be appointed to represent the child unless a guardian is not needed to safeguard the child's interests.

The guardian is an independent social worker, ie is not employed by the local authority involved in the proceedings.

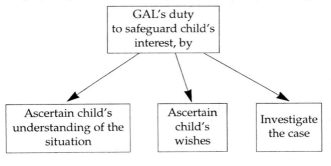

| To access LA record | To submit report to court | To appoint a solicitor if not done by the court |

Court can consider any aspect of report considered relevant regardless of act/rule of law making such evidence inadmissible

A solicitor may also be appointed by the guardian unless one has already been appointed by the court. He will give the solicitor instructions on the child's behalf unless the child has sufficient understanding to do so himself.

Emergency protection of children
Part V of the Children Act contains the measures intended to provide emergency protection for children. This part of the Act does not fall within the definition of 'family proceedings' and so the court will be unable to make s 8 orders when dealing with these applications.

When dealing with matters under Part V the court's decisions will be based on the welfare of the child being the paramount consideration, the delay principle and the 'no order' principle. It will not consider the matters contained in the checklist as it is dealing with a short-term remedy for an emergency situation.

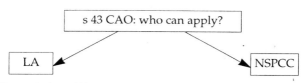

s 43 CAO: who can apply?

LA

NSPCC

Grounds (s 43(1)):

- the applicant has reasonable cause to suspect that the child is suffering or is likely to suffer significant harm;
- an assessment of the state of the child's health or development or of the way in which he has been treated is required to enable the applicant to determine whether or not the child is suffering or is likely to suffer significant harm; and
- it is unlikely that such an assessment will be made or be satisfactory in the absence of an order under this section.

The court will base its decision on the child's welfare and the order will require the parents or carers to produce the child for assessment or allow the child to be visited to allow an assessment to be carried out. This means that the child can remain with the family whilst any assessment is carried out. If the child has to go elsewhere for assessment, eg a hospital, and has to stay away from home for a few days then the court can give directions as to contact and may specify the length of time he can be kept there.

Child assessment order requirements

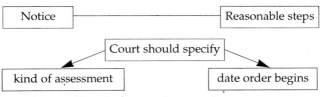

Notice — Reasonable steps

Court should specify

kind of assessment

date order begins

Duration: seven days maximum.

It should also specify how to make the assessment but a child of sufficient understanding can refuse to undergo any form of assessment contained in the order (s 43(8)).

If the parents refuse to comply with the assessment order there appears to be no direct form of enforcement. However, the local authority could inform them that if they continue to fail to comply with the order it could lead to the authority making an application for an emergency protection order.

An important point to bear in mind when considering whether or not to grant an assessment order is that if the court thinks that the grounds exist for the granting of an emergency protection order then the court may treat the application as an application for an emergency protection order and grant the order if the grounds are shown to exist (s 43(4)).

Emergency protection orders

The court will grant the order if it is satisfied that there is reasonable cause to believe that the child is likely to suffer significant harm if either:

- he is not removed to accommodation provided by or on behalf of the applicant; or

- he does not remain in the place where he is then being accommodated.

Although this section allows 'any person' to apply in practice it will usually be a local authority making the application.

The local authority may also apply under s 44(1)(b) when the court must be satisfied that:

- enquiries are being made in respect of the child under s 47(1)(b) (ie where the authority has the duty to investigate whether a child is suffering or is likely to suffer significant harm); and

- those enquiries are being frustrated by access to the child being unreasonably refused to a person authorised to seek access and that the applicant has reasonable cause to believe that access to the child is a matter of urgency.

Applications made by the NSPCC can also be made on similar grounds contained in s 44(1)(c).

Application made to family proceedings court. Duration: eight days + one extension only allowed of seven days.

The effects of an emergency protection order (EPO)

Section 44(4) allows the court to direct any person who is in a position to do so to produce the child to the applicant and authorises the removal to, or retention in, accommodation provided by the applicant, or prevents the removal of the child from some other place where the child was being accommodated immediately prior to the order.

It is an offence to prevent the removal of the child or to obstruct a person exercising the power to remove the child.

```
┌─────────────────────┐
│   Court can direct   │
└─────────────────────┘
     ╱        │        ╲
```

┌──────────────────────┐ ┌──────────────┐ ┌──────────────┐
│ Assessment, medical/ │ │   No   │ │   Contact   │
│ psychiatric (child can│ │ assessment │ │   with   │
│ refuse if of sufficient│ │ be made   │ │ parents etc │
│ understanding)   │ │   │ │   │
└──────────────────────┘ └──────────────┘ └──────────────┘

EPO gives applicant PR for duration of the order but
limits its use to safeguarding the child's welfare.

The authority should only remove the child from his home
for as long as is necessary for the child's welfare and should
return him home as soon as it is safe to do so. However, if
the applicant considers that he needs to remove the child
again during the existence of the order then he has the
power to do so.

No appeal against EPO
Application to discharge available after 72 hours.

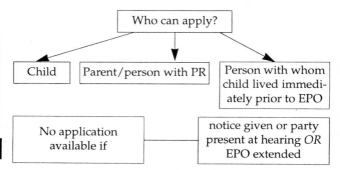

Wardship and the inherent jurisdiction

The wardship jurisdiction of the court is used to protect the interests of children and parental responsibility for the child rests with the court. If wardship is granted then the child will often stay with the party that made the application, but that party will not be able to take any important step in the child's life without the consent of the court, which can also give directions to safeguard the welfare of the child (*Re S* (1967)).

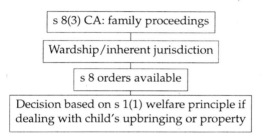

The inherent jurisdiction of the High Court is the use of the power of the Crown as *parens patriae*. This stems from the duty of the Crown to protect its subjects. The inherent jurisdiction is theoretically without limit but in practice there are limits which apply. Where the inherent jurisdiction applies to children it gives the court the ability to exceed the powers and overrule the decisions of parents and '*Gillick* competent' children (*Re W (A Minor) (Consent to Medical Treatment)* (1993)).

The inherent jurisdiction exists independently of wardship and can be used to protect the interests of a child which has not been made a ward. It is generally used to settle a specific issue, very often a medical matter, and will be used when there are no statutory provisions available to settle the issue.

Wardship and the Children Act 1989

The Children Act has, as we have seen, introduced a flexible range of orders which are available to the court when dealing with 'family proceedings'. This has made the use of wardship much less likely than previously and generally it will only be necessary in cases where the orders are unavailable.

Private law matters

The Children Act has not placed any restriction on the use of wardship in private law matters. However, the wide range of powers in s 8 of the Act makes it more likely that the parties will use these orders rather than use wardship.

There will be times when there could be an advantage to using wardship. If there is a leave requirement under the Children Act, the use of wardship will avoid this. Also if the element of continuing judicial control is thought to be necessary then again wardship will be the better route to take (*Re G-U (A Minor) (Wardship)* (1984)).

Public law matters

Unlike private law matters the area of public law has been severely restricted by the Children Act. Section 100(2) ensures that local authorities are no longer allowed to use wardship or the inherent jurisdiction to take children into care or make them subject to a supervision order.

However, there are situations when local authorities are still able to use the inherent jurisdiction albeit with the leave of the court (s 100(3)).

To grant leave the court must be satisfied that:

- the result that the local authority wishes to achieve could not be achieved by the making of any other type of order which the local authority might be entitled to apply for under the statutory code; and

- there is reasonable cause to believe that if the court's inherent jurisdiction is not exercised with respect to the child he is likely to suffer significant harm.

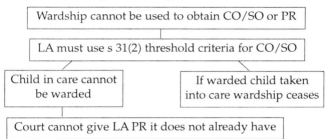

Wardship cannot be used to obtain CO/SO or PR

LA must use s 31(2) threshold criteria for CO/SO

Child in care cannot be warded

If warded child taken into care wardship ceases

Court cannot give LA PR it does not already have

Wardship applications

Wardship proceedings begin with originating summons in Family Division at High Court: minor warded when summons issued.

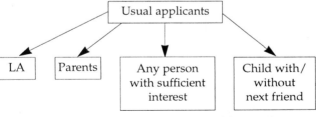

Usual applicants

LA | Parents | Any person with sufficient interest | Child with/without next friend

The type of situation which occurs in wardship is often concerned with medical matters and with decisions as to whether or not medical treatment is to be performed on the child. (Compare the cases of *Re Baby J* (1990) and *Re B (A Minor) (Wardship: Medical Treatment)* (1981)).

Publicity

In wardship proceedings, the court has the power to make an injunction prohibiting the publication of information which is considered harmful to the child. Any order made is binding on every person who is potentially subject to the order even though they have not been joined as a party to the proceedings.

Although the publication of information relating to proceedings before any court sitting in private is not in itself a contempt, there are exceptions to this situation which include:

- proceedings which relate to the exercise of the inherent jurisdiction of the High Court in relation to minors;

- proceedings under the Children Act 1989.

- any other proceedings which relate wholly or mainly to the maintenance or upbringing of a minor.

When deciding such matters the court will NOT regard the welfare of the child as paramount but it will regard the child's welfare as the most important consideration. The balance the court will seek to achieve when reaching its decision will be between that of the welfare of the child and that of the public interest (*Re H (Minors) (Injunction: Public Interest)* (1993)).

Adoption

The legislation covering the matter of adoption is contained in the Adoption Act 1976.

An adoption order brings a legal adoption into being and ends a natural parent's parental responsibility and vests it in the adoptive parents. It also ends any parental responsibility that any other person may have had for the child and brings to an end any order made under the Children Act 1989. However, such proceedings fall within the definition of 'family proceedings' and as such the court will be able to make use of s 8 orders in such proceedings should they consider them necessary.

Adoption agencies are responsible for arranging adoptions unless the prospective adopter is a relative or a person acting under a High Court order. Adoption agencies are run by local authorities or approved voluntary adoption societies and in practice most local authorities will run the service within its area.

The welfare of the child
Section 6 of the Adoption Act 1976 states that:

> In reaching any decision in relation to the adoption of a child a court or adoption agency must have regard to all the circumstances, first consideration being given to the need to safeguard and promote the welfare of the child throughout his childhood; and shall so far as practicable ascertain the wishes and feelings of the child regarding the decision and give due consideration to them, having regard to his age and understanding.

Thus it must be noted that the child's welfare is not paramount but is the first consideration.

Freeing for adoption
Section 18(1) of the Adoption Act allows an adoption agency to apply to the court for a 'freeing order' which declares that the child is free for adoption.

| Who can apply? | Only LAs can apply as adoption agencies as they only apply to children in care |

If granted, adoption agency gets PR, ends CA orders. Parents cannot veto adoption, allowing future planning. Consent required from parents/guardians with PR.

The consent of the unmarried father is not required but the court must be satisfied that he does not intend to apply for a parental responsibility order or for a residence order (RO) or that if he did make such an application it would be likely to be refused.

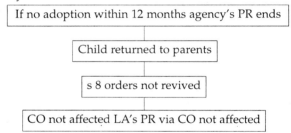

If no adoption within 12 months agency's PR ends

Child returned to parents

s 8 orders not revived

CO not affected LA's PR via CO not affected

Adoption order

When the court makes an adoption order it extinguishes the parental responsibility of the natural parents and gives it to the adoptive parents (s 12(1)).

When it decides whether or not to make an adoption order the court must apply the provisions of s 6 but may not make an order unless it is satisfied that sufficient opportunities to see the child together with one or both the applicants for the order in the home environment has been afforded to an officer of the responsible body.

Who can apply?

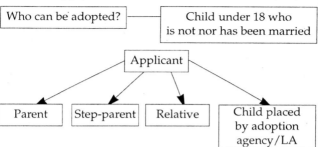

| Who can be adopted? | Child under 18 who is not nor has been married |

Applicant

Parent — Step-parent — Relative — Child placed by adoption agency/LA

Child must be over 19 weeks old and have lived with applicants for preceding 13 weeks.

| Other applicants | Child must be over 12 months old and have lived with applicants for previous 12 months |

Who can adopt?

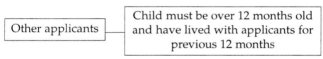

| Joint application | → | Married couples both over 21 years. If one party a parent then that person need only be over 18 years |

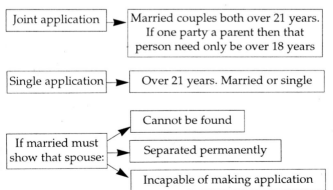

| Single application | → | Over 21 years. Married or single |

If married must show that spouse:	→	Cannot be found
	→	Separated permanently
	→	Incapable of making application

Parental agreement

Before court can make an adoption order, must have agreement of parent/guardian of the child.

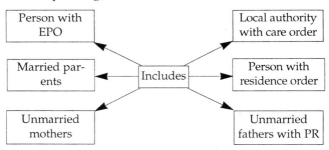

Person with EPO		Local authority with care order
Married parents	Includes	Person with residence order
Unmarried mothers		Unmarried fathers with PR

The mother of the child cannot give an effective consent until at least six weeks after the birth of her child (s 18(4)).

The court must be satisfied that the consent is freely given with full understanding of the situation and is unconditional, and this is witnessed by the reporting officer who will also provide the court with a full report on the case.

Criteria for granting adoption order

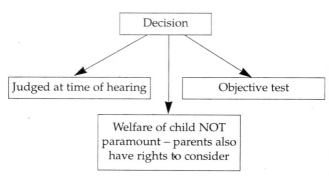

However, there will be times when the court will consider it necessary to dispense with parental agreement.

Grounds for dispensing with parental agreement
The grounds are contained in s 16(2).

They are when a parent or guardian:

- cannot be found or is incapable of giving agreement;
- is withholding his agreement unreasonably;
- has persistently failed without reasonable cause to discharge his parental responsibility for the child;
- has abandoned or neglected the child;
- has persistently ill-treated the child;
- has seriously ill-treated the child.

Parent cannot be found or is incapable of giving consent
In these circumstances enquiries must be made in an effort to trace the relevant persons to give them notice of the proposed adoption. If they cannot be found then their consent can be dispensed with. This is also permitted where their whereabouts are known but they cannot be contacted as in the case of *Re R (Adoption)* (1966). The parents could not be contacted due to the nature of the political regime in their country.

In *Re L (A Minor) (Adoption: Parental Agreement)* (1987) it was held that the natural mother was incapable of giving her consent as she was suffering from a mental disorder under the Mental Health Act 1983 and was unable to understand the consequences of the adoption.

Parent is withholding his agreement unreasonably
When considering this ground the court must bear in mind that just the fact that the parent does not agree with the proposed adoption will not make it unreasonable. A number of

considerations have to be kept in mind when deciding whether or not it is unreasonable.

The decision must be judged at the time of the hearing and an objective test used, ie would a reasonable parent withhold their consent? Also it must be remembered that the child's welfare is not to be considered as paramount, as in this situation the parent is in danger of losing his parental responsibility and rights in respect of the child and must be able to intervene if he has reasonable grounds to do so and as such the child's welfare is not allowed to override all other factors.

Having said that the welfare is not paramount, it must be seen as the most important factor and any reasonable parent would see it as such and would look to see if the child would benefit from adoption and if obvious advantages would arise then perhaps the parent should not withhold his consent.

However, just because a parent withholds his agreement it does not make it unreasonable. There can be any number of views taken by any number of people to a given situation and none of them need be unreasonable; they may be right or wrong but not necessarily unreasonable.

The court has to decide whether or not the decision on the case falls within this 'band' of reasonableness.

Compare the cases of *Re PA (An Infant)* (1971) and *Re D (An Infant) (Adoption: Parental Consent)* (1977).

Parent has persistently failed without reasonable cause to discharge his parental responsibility for the child

This factor includes the statutory duty on the parent to maintain the child and also to show the normal love and affection expected from a parent to a child.

Both elements of this ground must be satisfied, ie the element of persistence and the element of 'without just cause'.

The element of 'persistence' must be seen in the sense of being permanent and complete to such a degree that there would be no advantage to the child in maintaining contact with the parent as was held in the case of *Re B (S) (An Infant) (No 2)* (1968) where a father had not sought access to the child for a number of years and had failed to enquire about her or to maintain her during that period.

The court held that he had washed his hands of her and dispensed with his consent.

Re M (An Infant) (1965) illustrates that where an unmarried mother had left her child with the proposed adopters to conceal the birth from her parents it was seen by the court that she had failed to carry out her parental duties 'with just cause'.

Parent has abandoned or neglected the child

'Abandoned' in this sense would be equated with conduct which could render the parent liable to prosecution under the criminal law and is restrictively interpreted, as is the term 'neglected'. Because of this approach this factor is rarely used in practice.

Parent has persistently ill treated the child

'Persistent' is treated as in the above factor, ie permanent and in the case of *Re A (A Minor) (Adoption: Dispensing with Agreement)* (1981) it was held that a child that had been severely and repeatedly assaulted over a three-week period had been persistently ill treated.

Parent has seriously ill treated the child

Under this ground a single incident could lead the court to dispense with parental agreement if of a sufficiently serious nature, eg an incident of sexual abuse.

Proposals for reform

Proposals for reform in the area of adoption have been published in the consultation paper *Review of Adoption Law: Report to Ministers of an Inter-Departmental Working Group* and in the government White Paper *Adoption: The Future*.

8 Divorce reform

Criticisms of present system

Over recent years there has been growing dissatisfaction with the law concerning divorce in this country and the seemingly ever-increasing number of divorces which now stand at approximately 160,000 per annum. The main criticisms of the present system are that it:

- allows marriages to be ended too quickly and easily without the parties having to have regard to the consequences and effects on others of their actions;

- does little to try and preserve marriages that are in difficulty;

- does little to try and diminish any adverse effects or trauma suffered by the children of the family;

- increases the bitterness and hostility between the parties;

- is misleading and confusing;

- is open to abuse. Adultery and behaviour are used in approximately 80% of divorces, but often false allegations are used to facilitate the granting of the divorce;

- can be used to distort the parties' bargaining positions, eg matters regarding the children being used as bargaining ploys.

The Law Commission published *Facing the Future: A Discussion Paper on the Ground For Divorce*, and *Family Law: The Ground for Divorce*, which contained their proposals for the reform of divorce law. The main aims of these proposals were:

- to support and save marriages capable of being saved;

- to enable those not 'saveable' to be dissolved with the minimum of distress, hostility and bitterness;

- to encourage as far as is possible the amicable resolution of matters concerning finance, housing, children and their responsibilities to each other;

- to prevent or minimise the harm and distress to any children of the family during and after the divorce and to promote the continued sharing of parental responsibility and other responsibilities or duties towards the children.

The Lord Chancellor's Department published the Green Paper *Looking to the Future: Mediation and the Ground for Divorce*. This document showed that the Government's aims were somewhat different to those of the Law Commission in certain aspects and in emphasis in others. The Government's aims were:

- to support the institution of marriage;

- to include practicable steps to prevent the irretrievable breakdown of marriages;

- to ensure that the parties involved understand the practical consequences of divorce before taking any irreversible decisions;

- where divorce is unavoidable to minimise any bitterness and hostility between the parties and to reduce the trauma for the children involved;

- to keep to a minimum the cost to the parties and the taxpayer.

As we have seen in Chapter 2, the law on divorce at present is mainly contained in the Matrimonial Causes Act 1973.

However, it is anticipated that the Family Law Act 1996 will come into effect on 1 January 1999. This Act will repeal certain sections of the MCA and will no longer require the party seeking a divorce to prove one or more of the five facts bringing about the 'no fault' divorce system which had been sought earlier but only partially achieved by the earlier legislation.

Under the MCA the sole ground for divorce is the irretrievable breakdown of the marriage and this remains the situation under the Family Law Act. However the irretrievable breakdown is to be proved over a period of time rather than the use of the five facts.

As yet we have little or no indication as to how the new measures will be put into effect in practice or how the existing case law will apply, if at all, and students should read the commentaries that will be appearing in the near future as they will give much needed guidance.

Family Law Act 1996

Part I

Part I contains the principles of Parts II and III and the aims of the legislation. They are:

- that the institution of marriage is to be supported;

- that the parties to a marriage which may have broken down are to be encouraged to take all practicable steps whether by marriage counselling or otherwise to save the marriage;

- that a marriage which has irretrievably broken down and is being brought to an end should be brought to an end:

    o with the minimum distress to the parties and to any children affected;

- o with questions being dealt with in a manner designed to promote as good a continuing relationship between the parties and any children affected as is possible in the circumstances; and

- o without costs being unreasonably incurred in connection with the procedures to be followed in bringing the marriage to an end;

- that any risk to one of the parties to a marriage or to any children of violence from the other party should as far as reasonably practicable be removed or diminished.

Part II

Divorce and separation

This part deals with the power of the courts to make divorce orders and separation orders and the circumstances in which they may be made.

Divorce orders dissolve the marriage and separation orders provide for the separation of the parties. Both orders come into effect on being made and separation orders will continue while the marriage continues or until cancelled by the court on the joint application of the parties.

Availability of divorce/separation orders

The circumstances in which such orders can be made, on an application by one or both parties, are:

- the marriage has broken down irretrievably;

- the requirements of s 8 (information meetings) are satisfied;

- the requirements of s 9 (future arrangements) are satisfied;

- the application has not been withdrawn.

However, no divorce order may be made if an order preventing divorce is in force under s 10 – the hardship bar. This is similar to that contained in s 5 of the MCA but also covers the relevant child.

If an application for a divorce order (DO) is being considered and an application for a separation order is made in respect of the same marriage, the court will deal with the case as if only a divorce order application was being made unless:

- a s 10 order is in force;

- a s 10 order is made;

- s 7(6) or (13) applies.

Under s 7(6) there can be no application for a divorce order prior to the first anniversary of the marriage and under s 7(13) the period of reflection and consideration has been extended.

A separation order (SO) can be converted into a divorce order if s 11 requirements (children's welfare) are met, but there are some restrictions. A separation order cannot be converted prior to the second anniversary of the marriage. Also it cannot be converted if:

- there is a s 10 order in force; OR

- if there is a child of the family under the age of 16 when the application is made; OR

- there has been an application for the period of reflection and consideration to be extended.

However, the second two points above will not apply if at the time of the application there is an occupation order or a non-molestation order in force in favour of the applicant or a child of the family against the other party.

Also, the second two points above will cease to apply if the six-month extension to the period of reflection and consideration ends OR there ceases to be a child under 16 years of age.

Availability of divorce/separation orders

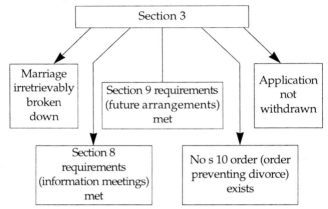

Marital breakdown

As stated earlier, the sole ground for divorce will still be the irretrievable breakdown of the marriage and this will be shown by:

- a statement made by one or both parties that the maker(s) believe that the marriage has broken down;

- that the statement complies with the requirements of s 6;

- that the period of reflection and consideration has ended;

- the application under s 3 is accompanied by a declaration by the party making the application that:

  o having reflected on the breakdown; AND

- ○ having considered the requirements of Part II as to the parties' arrangements for the future

- the applicant believes that the marriage cannot be saved.

It is not necessary for the party making the statement to be the party making the application.

No application for a divorce order can be made by reference to a s 3 statement if:

- the parties give joint notice of withdrawal of the statement; OR

- a period of one year has passed since the end of the period of reflection and consideration. This is known as the 'specified period'.

When calculating this period no account will be taken of any period during which there was a s 10 order in being. Also if the parties give joint notice that they are attempting a reconciliation and require additional time then the specified period stops running from the day that joint notice is received by the court but will resume on the day the court receives notice from either party that the attempted reconciliation has failed. If this period of interruption lasts for a continuous period of over 18 months then a new statement will be required before any application can be made.

The statement of marital breakdown may be made by either or both parties and it must state that the maker of the statement is aware of the purpose of the period of reflection and consideration and the need to make arrangements for the future.

No statement made prior to the first anniversary of the marriage can be used for an application for a divorce order.

Irretrievable breakdown

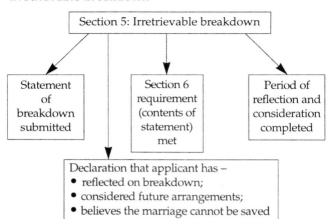

```
┌─────────────────────────────────────────┐
│    Section 5: Irretrievable breakdown    │
└─────────────────────────────────────────┘
```

Statement of breakdown submitted	Section 6 requirement (contents of statement) met	Period of reflection and consideration completed

Declaration that applicant has –
- reflected on breakdown;
- considered future arrangements;
- believes the marriage cannot be saved

Reflection and consideration

The period for reflection and consideration is for the parties to reflect on whether the marriage can be saved and to have an opportunity to effect a possible reconciliation or, if this is not possible, to consider what arrangements should be made for the future.

The period begins 14 days after the statement of marital breakdown is received by the court. It will last for a minimum of nine months but can be extended for a further six months if a party applies for further time for reflection and consideration or there is a child of the family under 16 years. If the period is extended because of the presence of such a child the extension will end when there ceases to be any children under 16 years.

However such an extension will not be available if at the time of an application for a divorce order there is an occupation order or non-molestation order in force in favour of the applicant or a child of the family against the other party, or the court is satisfied that delaying the making of a divorce order would be significantly detrimental to the welfare of any child of the family.

The court may also extend the period if there has been undue delay in the service of documentation and the other party applies for an extension but it cannot be extended beyond the period between the beginning of the period and the time of service.

An application for a divorce order or a separation order can only be made after the completion of the period of reflection and consideration.

The parties can interrupt this period by giving joint notice to the court that they are attempting a reconciliation (R/C) and require further time for reflection and consideration. The period will stop running on the day the notice is received by the court but resumes when notice is received from either party that the attempt has been unsuccessful. If this period of interruption is continuous for over 18 months then a new statement of marital breakdown will be required.

Time periods to be met during DO/SO procedure

TIMETABLE		
INFORMATION MEETING	——	0
STATEMENT OF MARITAL BREAKDOWN	——	3 MONTHS
STATEMENT SERVED/FILED	——	14 DAYS
PERIOD OF R/C BEGINS		
MINIMUM PERIOD PRIOR TO APPLICATION FOR DO/SO	——	9 MONTHS
PERIOD OF R/C EXTENDED IF: • Child under 16 yrs • Party applies for further time for R/C	——	6 MONTHS MAXIMUM
SPECIFIED PERIOD TO APPLY FOR DO/SO AFTER PERIOD OF R/C	——	12 MONTHS

Information meetings

However, before the original statement of marital breakdown can be submitted to the court, the party wishing to make the statement must have attended an information meeting at least three months prior to making the statement.

If the statement is made jointly then the parties must have attended meetings either together or separately.

If only one party makes the statement then the other party must attend a meeting prior to making applications in respect of a child of the family or certain matters relating to property or financial matters or contesting such matters.

Information meetings are intended to provide relevant information on matters which may arise in connection with Parts II or III of the Act and to give those attending a meeting the opportunity to meet with a marriage counsellor and indeed to encourage the couple to do so.

The information which should be given in such meetings must cover:

- marriage counselling and other marriage support services;
- the importance to be attached to the welfare, wishes and feelings of children;
- how the parties may acquire a better understanding of the ways in which children can be helped to cope with the breakdown of the marriage;
- the nature of the financial questions which may arise on divorce or separation and services which are available to help the parties;
- protection available against violence and how to obtain support and assistance;
- mediation;
- the availability to each of the parties of independent legal advice and representation;
- the principles of legal aid and where the parties can get advice about obtaining legal aid;
- the divorce and separation process.

Although these matters are set out in the Act, how they will be dealt with in practice will depend a great deal on the findings of the pilot schemes which are to be set up in parts of the country. The practical difficulties these schemes will uncover will provide the guidance to allow the necessary regulations to be made.

Arrangements for the future

A s 3 application requires that the requirements of s 9 are satisfied. Section 9(2) states that one of the following must be produced to the court:

(a) a court order (made by consent or otherwise) dealing with their financial arrangements;

(b) consent order;

(c) contested litigation reaching agreement in either–
  (i)   a consent order; or
  (ii) a negotiated settlement;

(d) a declaration by one of the parties (to which no objection has been notified to the court by the other party) that–
  (i)   he has no significant assets and does not intend to make an application for financial provision;
  (ii) he believes that the other party has no significant assets and does not intend to make an application for financial provision; and
  (iii) there are therefore no financial arrangements to be made.

Also the arrangements for the welfare of the children must be satisfied.

There are, however, exemptions contained in Schedule 1 which allow the court to make orders, even if the contents of s 9(2) have not been satisfied, if a party applies at the end of the period of reflection and consideration.

Exemptions to required arrangements for the future

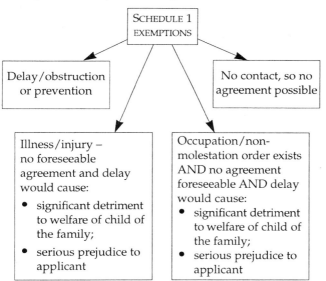

Orders preventing divorce

Section 10 contains provisions relating to orders preventing divorce. This measure is similar to the hardship bar contained in s 5 MCA 1973.

If an application is made for a divorce order then the court may, on an application by the other party, make an order preventing divorce.

The court must be satisfied that:

- that the dissolution of the marriage would result in substantial financial or other hardship to the other party or to a child of the family;

- that it would be wrong in all the circumstances (including the conduct of the parties and the interests of any child of the family) for the marriage to be dissolved.

An application to cancel such an order made by one or both the parties will allow the court to cancel the order unless the considerations still apply.

After a cancellation is made then a further application for a divorce order must be made.

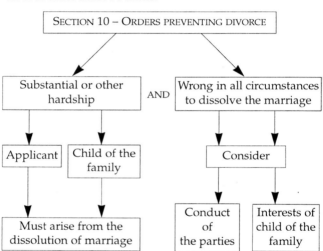

The welfare of the children

A significant change from the MCA, where the welfare of the child of the family was the first consideration, is to be found in s 11(3) where it states that where the court considers whether or not the circumstances of the case require or are likely to require the use of its powers under the Children Act 1989 then the welfare of the child is paramount.

This consideration and whether there are any children to whom s 11 applies are to be considered in any application for a divorce order or a separation order.

Resolution of disputes

After receiving a statement, the court may give directions that each party should attend a meeting arranged for an explanation of facilities for mediation with regard to their dispute and provide an opportunity for each party to agree to take advantage of these facilities.

Such a direction can be given at any time, including in the course of proceedings connected with the breakdown of the marriage, on application, or on the initiative of the court.

'Connected proceedings'

Section 25(2): any proceedings under Parts I to V Children Act 1989 with respect to a child of the family or any proceedings resulting from an application:

- for or for the cancellation of an order preventing divorce in relation to the marriage;

- by either party to the marriage for an order under Part IV;

- for the exercise in relation to a party to the marriage or child of the family of any of the court's powers under Part II MCA 1973;

- made otherwise to the court with respect to or in connection with any proceedings connected with the breakdown of the marriage.

The parties are required to attend the same meeting unless one or both ask for separate meetings or the court considers separate meetings to be more appropriate.

Following the basic aims of the Act the court has power to adjourn proceedings to allow the parties to comply with a mediation direction or to enable them to resolve disputes amicably. The court will consider the need to protect the interests of any child of the family when deciding on any adjournment.

Financial provision

Schedule 2 amends the MCA 1973 and its main aim is to allow financial provision to be made in cases of divorce orders and separation orders before such orders are made but to retain the position in cases where marriages are annulled.

Section 22A MCA deals with financial provision in divorce and separation cases. The basic orders will remain as at present, ie periodic payments, lump sums and property adjustment orders but as the arrangements for the future requirements in s 9 show the parties should have dealt with such matters and hopefully reached an amicable arrangement that the court could accept.

The court can make such orders at the appropriate time in favour of:

- a party to the marriage;
- a child of the family.

Section 22B MCA deals with restrictions on such cases.

No orders, other than interim orders, are to take effect prior to the making of a divorce order or a separation order unless:

- the circumstances of the case are exceptional; or
- that it would be just and reasonable to do so.

Also the court will be unable to make such orders during a period of interruption of reflection and consideration. In addition, no order can be made under s 22A after the granting of a divorce order or during the existence of a separation order unless:

- the application was made before the order;

- a subsequent application was made with the leave of the court.

Section 23 MCA deals with financial provision in nullity cases.

Here interim orders are available to the court prior to the decree absolute, but the main orders only take effect after the decree absolute.

Section 23A MCA deals with property adjustment orders in divorce and separation cases.

The orders concern the transfer of property, the settlement of property, the variation of settlements and the extinguishing or reducing the interests under a settlement.

Section 23B MCA deals with restrictions on such order and they are virtually the same as those in s 22B.

Section 24 deals with property adjustment orders in nullity cases.

The definitions for this area are contained in the new s 21 MCA.

An important aspect is that when the court is dealing with these matters, the discretion which existed under the MCA is retained and the court may make orders as it sees fit, and the considerations in s 25 remain unaltered other than for minor amendments as mentioned in Schedule 8.

There are also provisions for 'pension splitting' in s 16 and this new facility for the court will require regulations to be made which will need to be considered along with the Pensions Act 1995 and other proposed legislation.

Marriage support services

The Lord Chancellor may in future make grants for:

- the provision of marriage support services;
- research into causes of marital breakdown;
- research into ways of preventing marital breakdown.

However, these grants will need to be with the approval of the Treasury.

The Lord Chancellor may also provide marriage counselling but only when a period of reflection and consideration is running in relation to the marriage, or if a period of interruption (of less than 18 months) exists, and only to parties who would not be required to make any contributions towards the costs of mediation provided under Part IIIA of the Legal Aid Act 1988. Only those considered suitable for such services by a marriage counsellor will be provided with them.

Part III

Mediation and Legal Aid

The main purpose of mediation is seen as an attempt to lessen the harmful and distressing effects of divorce. The Law Commission said the aim was to 'help separating couples reach their own arrangements about the future, to improve communications between them and to help them co-operate in bringing up their own children'.

It illustrates a move away from adversarial procedures towards a more constructive system – the use of the period of reflection and consideration assisted by mediation.

The system would start with a personal interview which would supply the parties with information about the legal procedures and the consequences of divorce and inform them of the services which they may require. They would not, however, be given legal advice.

The parties would be encouraged to use mediation rather than lawyers as this would obviously cut the legal aid bill. However, some practitioners are of the opinion that even though mediation will be of value, it could be unwise for the parties to reach agreement on major issues without the benefit of legal advice. Where total or partial agreement is reached via mediation this could then either remain a private agreement enforceable as a contract or be enforced as a consent order, and it is envisaged that legal advice will still be required in either circumstance.

Another aim is to provide a better service at less cost to both the taxpayer and the parties but the basic policy is that the main cost of dissolving the marriage should fall on the parties. However, should this lead to unequal bargaining positions or cause a situation where children are put at risk then there will be an obvious case for financial assistance with costs.

Mediation will be available in relation to 'family matters' which are defined as:

- Matrimonial Causes Act 1973;
- Domestic Proceedings and Magistrates' Courts Act 1978;
- Parts I and V Children Act 1989;
- Parts II and IV Family Law Act 1996 and other prescribed enactments.

However, the regulations covering this provision can only be made with the approval of the Treasury.

Mediation will include the decision made by the mediator to:

- decide whether to embark on mediation;
- prepare for mediation;
- make any assessment.

Mediation will be provided to parties whose financial resources are such as to make them eligible for mediation but only if the mediator decides it is suitable to the dispute, the parties and all the circumstances.

If it is, then the parties will not be required to pay if he is legally aided, unless he is required to contribute to his legal aid in which case he will also be required to contribute to the cost of mediation.

There also exists the equivalent to the statutory charge. Where property is recovered or preserved for the legally aided party as a result of mediation a sum equal to the Board's liability is to be a first charge on the property in favour of the Board.

In connection with civil legal aid, no party will be granted representation for family matters unless he has attended a meeting with a mediator to decide if mediation is suitable and whether it could take place without either party being influenced by fear of violence or other harm, and if mediation appears suitable to help the party applying for representation to decide whether instead to apply for mediation. However, this restriction will not apply in relation to proceedings under:

- Part IV Family Law Act 1996;

- s 37 Matrimonial Causes Act 1973;

- Parts IV or V Children Act 1989.

The Legal Aid Board, when considering whether it is reasonable for a party to be represented:

- must have regard to whether and to what extent mediation would be a suitable alternative to taking proceedings; and

- must have regard to the outcome of the meeting held with the mediator and to any assessment made.

Part IV

Family homes and domestic violence

This part deals with the reform of the measures dealing with the difficult area of domestic violence which were previously contained in the Matrimonial Homes Act 1983, the Domestic Violence and Matrimonial Proceedings Act 1976, and the Domestic Proceedings and Magistrates Courts Act 1978.

In the case of *Richards v Richards* (1984) Scarman LJ described the situation as he saw it:

> The statutory provision is a hotchpotch of enactments of limited scope passed into law to meet specific situations or to strengthen the powers of specified courts. The sooner the range, scope and effect of these powers are rationalised into a coherent and comprehensive body of statute law the better.

The majority of the reforms were contained in the discussion paper No 113 *Domestic Violence and Occupation of the Family Home* published by the Law Commission and the *Report on Domestic Violence and Occupation of the Family Home*. The aims expressed by the Law Commission are:

The first is to remove the gaps, anomalies and inconsistencies in the existing remedies with a view to synthesising them, so far as is possible, into a clear, simple comprehensive code. Secondly, we have taken it for granted that any reform should not reduce the level of protection which is available at present and might wish to improve it. Thirdly, however, it is desirable and consistent with our work with children and divorce to seek to avoid exacerbating hostilities between the adults involved so far as this is compatible with providing proper and effective protection for both adults and for children.

It is hoped that these aims will be achieved through a single set of remedies available in all levels of court although there will have to be some limits on the powers of magistrates' courts.

Rights to occupy matrimonial home
Section 30(1) gives the non-estate holding spouse the right to occupy the matrimonial home if the other spouse is entitled to occupy by virtue of a beneficial estate or interest, contract or any enactment.

These matrimonial home rights are:

- if in occupation a right not to be evicted or excluded from the dwelling house or any part of it by the other spouse except with the leave of the court given by an order under s 33;

- if not in occupation, a right with the leave of the court so given to enter into and occupy the dwelling house.

Section 31 states that matrimonial home rights are a charge on the estate or interest of the other spouse and have the same priority as if an equitable interest has been created at whichever is the latest of:

- the date on which the spouse so entitled acquires the estate or interest;
- the date of the marriage; and
- 1 January 1968 (the commencement date of the Matrimonial Homes Act 1967).

Even though the matrimonial homes rights are a charge, these rights are brought to an end by the death of the other spouse or the termination of the marriage (other than by death) unless an order exists under s 33(5). The charge takes priority after an existing mortgage.

Occupation orders

Where a person is entitled to occupy a dwelling house by virtue of a beneficial estate or interest or contract or has matrimonial home rights (MHR) in relation to a dwelling house and that dwelling house is or has been or was intended to be the home of that person or another person associated with him then he can apply for an occupation order. A formerly engaged person can also apply for such an order, but such application must be made within three years of the termination of the engagement. The time runs from the day the engagement ends.

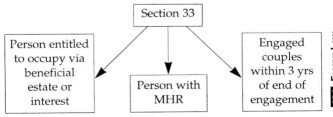

The order may:

- enforce the applicant's entitlement to remain in occupation as against the other person (the respondent);

- require the respondent to permit the applicant to enter and remain in the dwelling-house or part of the dwelling house;

- regulate the occupation of the dwelling house by either or both the parties;

- if the respondent is entitled by virtue of a beneficial estate or interest or contract, prohibit, suspend or restrict the exercise by him of his right to occupy the dwelling house;

- if the respondent has matrimonial home rights in relation to the dwelling house and the applicant is the other spouse, restrict or terminate those rights;

- require the respondent to leave the dwelling house or part of the dwelling house; or

- exclude the respondent from a defined area in which the dwelling house is included.

The important new measure here is the power to exclude the respondent from a defined area.

Effect of orders

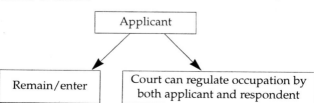

Respondent			
Prohibited/ suspended/ restricted	MHRs: restricted/ terminated	Required to leave	Excluded from a defined area

Further to these provisions, the court may also declare that the applicant is entitled to occupy the dwelling house because of a beneficial estate and interest or contract or has matrimonial home rights. Also s 33(5) allows the court to make an order extending the order beyond the death of the other spouse or the termination of the marriage.

The criteria for making a decision on occupation orders under subsection (3) are contained in subsection (6).

Subsection 7 illustrates the new attitude that now the order is expected to be made if it appears to the court that the applicant or a relevant child is likely to suffer significant harm attributable to the conduct of the respondent. It need not be made, however, if significant harm may be caused to the respondent and any relevant child and that this significant harm would be greater than that caused to the applicant or child if the order is not made. There is no mention of the order having to be 'just and reasonable'.

Criteria for occupation order

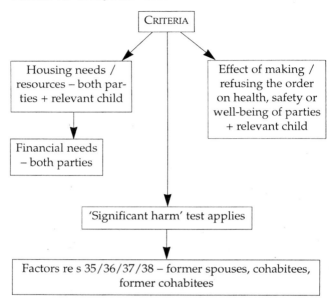

However, when the court is deciding whether to make an order under s 5 then the court will consider whether it is just and reasonable in all the circumstances to make such an order.

Occupation orders can be made for a specified period or until a further order but will cease on the death of either party and cannot be made after the death of either party.

Similar orders appear in s 35 but apply to former spouses. However when looking at the criteria in s 35(6) it will be seen that there are three extra factors to be borne in mind.

They are:

(e) the length of time that has elapsed since the parties ceased to live together;

(f) the length of time that has elapsed since the marriage was dissolved or annulled; and

(g) the existence of any pending proceedings between the parties–

  (i)   for an order under s 23A or s 24 of MCA 1973 (property adjustment orders in divorce, separation and nullity);

  (ii) for an order para 1(2)(d) or (e) of Sched 1 of Children Act 1989 (orders for financial relief against parents); or

  (iii) relating to the legal or beneficial ownership of the dwelling house.

Again there is a presumption that the order will be made unless the 'significant harm' test is satisfied as with spouses in s 35(7).

The orders in this area can be made for a specified period of up to six months and can be extended on one or more occasions for further periods not exceeding six months.

Section 36 also provides similar protection for cohabitants and former cohabitants with no existing rights to occupy. The orders in sub-ss 3 and 4 are as those for spouses.

However there are some differences in the criteria. In addition to those (a) to (d) as in s 35(6) there are:

(6) ...

(e) the nature of the parties' relationship;

(f) the length of time during which they have lived together as husband and wife;

(g) whether there are or have been any children who are children of both parties or for whom both parties have or have had parental responsibility;

(h) the length of time that has elapsed since the parties ceased to live together; and

(i) the existence of any pending proceedings between the parties–
    (i) for an order under para 1(2)(d) or (e) of Sched 1 Children Act 1989; or

    (ii) relating to the legal or beneficial ownership of the dwelling-house.

When deciding whether or not to make an order containing a sub-s 5 provision the court must consider factors (a)–(d) and the questions in sub-s 8 which equates with the 'significant harm test'.

An order made under this section can be made for a specified period not exceeding six months and may be extended on one occasion for a further period of up to six months.

Section 37 applies if either spouse or former spouse occupy a dwelling-house which is or was a matrimonial home but neither of them is entitled to remain in occupation by virtue of a beneficial estate or interest or contract. Either party may apply for an order against the other in similar terms to s 33. The same criteria will apply as will the 'significant' harm test and the order will last for up to six months and can be extended on one or more occasions for up to six months.

Section 38 applies to cohabitants or former cohabitants, neither of whom are entitled to occupy the matrimonial home. The criteria are as in s 36 (a) to (d) and the 'significant harm' test. Again the order can be made for up to six months with only one extension of up to six months.

Duration

s 33	Specified period/until further order

ss 35/37	6 mths max + 1 or more extensions – 6 mths max

s 36/38	6 mths max + 1 extension – 6 mths max

An occupation order can be made with or without other family proceedings.

If an application for an occupation order is made under s 33, 35, 36, 37 or 38 and the court considers that there is no power to make the order, then if it has the power, it may make an order under one of the other sections.

Where an occupation order is made under s 33, 35 or 36 then the court may, at the time or at any time after,

- impose obligations on either party to–

  o the repair and maintenance of the dwelling house; or

  o the discharge of rent, mortgage payments or other outgoings affecting the dwelling house;

- order the party occupying the dwelling house to make periodical payments to the other party in respect of the accommodation if the other party would (but for the order) be entitled to occupy the dwelling house by virtue of a beneficial estate or interest or contract;

- grant either party possession or use of furniture or other contents of the dwelling house;

- order either party to take reasonable care of any furniture or other contents of the dwelling house;

- order either party to take reasonable steps to keep the dwelling house and any furniture or other contents secure.

When deciding whether or not to make such an order the court must consider the financial needs and resources of the parties and the financial obligations they are likely to have in the foreseeable future, including financial obligations they would have to each other and any relevant child. Any such order would cease to have effect when the occupation order ends.

Obligations courts may apply to occupation orders

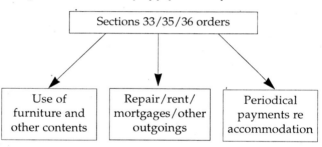

Section 41 contains an additional consideration where the parties concerned are cohabitants or former cohabitants and the court, where it has to consider the parties' relationship, must have regard to the fact that they have not given each other the commitment involved in marriage.

Transfer of tenancies

Another aspect of what arguably could be seen as protection, furthered by the Act in Schedule 7, is the ability of the courts to transfer certain types of tenancies on divorce or separation of cohabitants.

The types of tenancies which are included are:

- a protected tenancy or statutory tenancy within the meaning of the Rent Act 1977;

- a statutory tenancy within the meaning of the Rent (Agriculture) Act 1976;

- a secure tenancy within the meaning of s 79, Housing Act 1985; or

- an assured tenancy or assured agricultural occupancy within the meaning of Part I, Housing Act 1988.

The power is available to the court when one spouse is entitled to occupy a dwelling house by virtue of a relevant tenancy either in his own right or jointly with the other spouse and the court has power to make a property adjustment order under s 23A (divorce or separation) or under s 24 (nullity). It is also available with respect to cohabitants where there is entitlement as with spouses and the parties cease to live together as husband and wife.

The dwelling house in question must have been the matrimonial home for spouses or the home where cohabitants lived as husband and wife.

In deciding such matters the court shall have regard to all the circumstances of the case including:

- the circumstances in which the tenancy was granted to either or both the parties or the circumstances in which they became tenants under the tenancy;

- the matters mentioned in s 36(a)–(c) (needs and resources and considerations with respect to children) and where the parties are cohabitants and only one of them is entitled to occupy the dwelling house by virtue of the relevant tenancy the further matters mentioned in s 36(6)(e)–(h) (nature and length of relationship, children for whom they have had PR and how long they have lived apart); and

- the suitability of the parties as tenants. The court should also give the landlord of the dwelling house an opportunity to be heard.

Under Part II of this Schedule the court can direct that the tenancy can be transferred and vested in the other spouse, or if jointly held then to that spouse alone. Along with the tenancy will also be transferred all the privileges and obligations and liabilities and any indemnities.

Under Part III the court may order compensation to be paid to the transferor by the transferee but may defer such payment or allow payment by instalments. When deciding these matters the court will consider all the circumstances and–

- the financial loss to the transferor that would otherwise occur as a result of the order;

- the financial needs and resources of the parties;

- the financial obligations the parties have or are likely to have in the foreseeable future including such obligations to each other and any children.

However the ability to defer or allow instalments will only be available if to order immediate payment would cause the transferee financial hardship greater than that which would be suffered by the transferor if it was granted.

Even if the tenancy is transferred, the court may order that both parties should be jointly and severally liable for the discharge or performance of all obligations and liabilities in respect of the dwelling house which previously fell only to one of the parties. If such an order is made, the court may also direct that an indemnity by one party to the other be made for carrying out the obligations.

The appropriate time for transfers taking effect in the case of nullity is on the granting of the decree absolute and in the case of divorce or separation is the date to be determined as if the court was making a property adjustment under s 23A MCA.

No application for a transfer can be made by a spouse after the remarriage of that spouse.

Non-molestation orders

A non-molestation order is an order containing either or both the following provisions–

- prohibiting a person (the respondent) from molesting another person who is associated with the respondent;

- prohibiting the respondent from molesting a relevant child.

The definitions of 'relevant child' and 'associated' are contained in s 62(2) and (3)–(5) and should be known as the class of possible applicants for non-molestation orders has been significantly widened to provide greater protection in cases of domestic violence where the parties are not married. If an application is made by an associated person who was engaged to the respondent then the application must be made within three years of the end of the engagement.

Section 63 contains the definitions of the general terms used in this part of the Act.

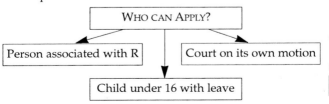

The court can make a non-molestation order–

- on application made by a person associated with the respondent (with or without other family proceedings); or

- if, in any family proceedings to which the respondent is a party, the court considers that the order should be made for the benefit of the other party to the proceedings or any relevant child even though no application has been made.

'Family proceedings' are defined as:

Proceedings under the inherent jurisdiction of the High Court in relation to children and the following enactments:

- Parts II and IV FLA 1996;

- MCA 1973;

- Adoption Act 1976;

- DPMCA 1978;

- Part III Matrimonial and Family Proceedings Act 1984;

- Parts I, II and IV Children Act 1989;

- Section 30 Human Fertilisation and Embryology Act 1990.

Also included is the amendment to the Children Act concerning the exclusion requirement that can now be added to an emergency protection order under s 44A.

A non-molestation order can be made to cover either particular or general molestation and can be made for a specified period or until further order. If the order is made within family proceedings then the order will cease to have effect when the family proceedings are withdrawn or dismissed.

The criteria the court will apply when determining the question of non-molestation orders are all the circumstances, including the need to secure the health, safety and well-being–

- of the applicant, or in the case falling within s 2(b), the person for whose benefit the order would be made; and

- of any relevant child.

A child under the age of 16 years cannot make an application for a non-molestation order without the leave of the court. The court may grant leave only if it considers that the child has sufficient understanding to make the application for an occupation order or non-molestation order.

An occupation order or non-molestation order may be varied or discharged by the court on application by the respondent or the person on whose application the order was made. In the case of non-molestation orders the court could vary or discharge the order on its own motion.

Criteria for granting non-molestation orders

All the circumstances of the case including the need to secure the health, safety and well-being of

Applicant or person for whose benefit order made

Relevant child

As the need for protection from violence can arise in emergencies there could be a need for *ex parte* orders and the court has the power in s 45. Occupation orders and non-molestation orders can be granted if the court considers that it is just and convenient.

When deciding these matters the court will consider all the circumstances including:

- any risk of significant harm to the applicant or a relevant child attributable to the conduct of the respondent, if the order is not made immediately; and

- whether it is likely that the applicant will be deterred or prevented from pursuing the application if an order is not made immediately; and

- whether there is reason to believe that the respondent is aware of the proceedings but is deliberately evading service and that the applicant or a relevant child will be seriously prejudiced by the delay involved–

  o where the court is a magistrates court in effecting service of proceedings; or

  o in any other case in effecting substituted service.

The court must allow the respondent an opportunity to make representations at a full hearing as soon as is just and convenient. If at the full hearing the court makes an occupation order then as regards the period of six months the time will run from the making of the initial order as will the provisions regarding extensions.

Powers of arrest

Under s 47 the court, on making an occupation order or a non-molestation order, where it appears that the respondent has used or threatened violence against the applicant or relevant child, shall attach a power of arrest to one or more of the provisions of the order unless it is satisfied that the applicant or child will be adequately protected without such a power. Thus there is a presumption that there will be a power of arrest attached. This is not the position at present.

This does not apply to *ex parte* orders, but the court can attach a power of arrest if it is satisfied that the respondent has used or threatened violence against the applicant or relevant child and there is a risk of significant harm to the applicant or relevant child attributable to the conduct of the respondent if the power of arrest is not attached to the provisions immediately.

If the power of arrest is attached then a constable may arrest without warrant a person whom he has reasonable cause for suspecting to be in breach of any such provision. A person who is arrested must be brought before the relevant judicial authority within 24 hours and if the matter is not disposed of then he may be remanded.

If the court has made an order but has not attached a power of arrest or has only attached the power to certain provisions of the order then if the applicant considers that the respondent has failed to comply with the order, he may apply to the court for the issue of a warrant for the arrest of the respondent. The court may only issue the warrant if satisfied that the application is substantiated on oath and has reasonable grounds for believing that the respondent has failed to comply with the order.

Available if R has used/threatened to use violence against applicant/relevant child	Shall be attached unless adequate protection without the power

If no power of arrest attached and applicant considers R has failed to comply with order applicant can seek warrant.

In any case where the court can make occupation orders or non-molestation orders the court may accept an undertaking from any party to the proceedings and no power of arrest can be attached to an undertaking. However, the court shall not accept an undertaking in any case where, apart from this restriction, a power of arrest would be attached.

Amendments to Children Act 1989

Another important addition to the protective powers available to the courts has been introduced by amendments to the Children Act in Schedule 6. Under s 38A Children Act, where the court is satisfied that the requirements for an interim care order have been met, the court may include an exclusion requirement if:

(a) there is reasonable cause to believe that if a person (the relevant person) is excluded from a dwelling house in which the child lives the child will cease to suffer or cease to be likely to suffer significant harm; and

(b) another person living in the dwelling house (whether a parent of the child or some other person)—

   (i) is able and willing to give to the child the care which it would be reasonable to expect a parent to give him and

   (ii) consents to the inclusion of the exclusion requirement.

The court has the power to attach the power of arrest to an exclusion requirement. A constable may arrest without warrant any person whom he has reasonable cause to believe to be in breach of the requirement.

If while the interim care order with an exclusion requirement is in force the local authority removes the child from the dwelling house from which the relevant person is excluded for a continuous period of more than 24 hours, the exclusion requirement of the order will cease to have effect. If the court accepts an undertaking in place of making an exclusion requirement then no power of arrest can be attached.

Under s 44A Children Act 1989 there is also now the ability to attach an exclusion requirement to an emergency protection order if the court is satisfied that:

(a) there is reasonable cause to believe that if a person(the relevant person) is excluded from a dwelling house in which the child lives then–

  (i) in the case of an order made on the ground mentioned in s 44(1)(a) the child will not be likely to suffer significant harm even though the child is not removed as mentioned in s 44(1)(a)(i) or does not remain as mentioned in s 44(1)(a)(ii); or

  (ii) in the case of an order made on the ground mentioned in para (b) or (c) of s 44(1) the enquiries referred to in that paragraph will cease to frustrated; and

(b) that another person living in the dwelling house (whether a parent of the child or some other person)–

  (i) is able and willing to give to the child the care which it would be reasonable to expect a parent to give him and

  (ii) consents to the inclusion of the exclusion requirement.

The factors dealing with the power of arrest is as the case with the interim care order, as is the situation with undertakings. Also the definition of an exclusion requirement is common to both sections–

(a) a provision requiring the relevant person to leave a dwelling house in which he is living with the child;

(b) a provision prohibiting the relevant person from entering a dwelling house in which the child lives;

(c) a provision excluding the relevant person from a defined area in which the dwelling house in which the child lives is situated.

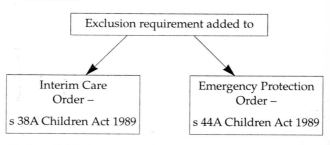

Exclusion requirement added to

Interim Care Order –

s 38A Children Act 1989

Emergency Protection Order –

s 44A Children Act 1989

Both end if LA removes child from dwelling-house from where R excluded for a continuous period of over 24 hours.

Power of arrest factors apply.

As can be seen from the information contained in this chapter, there is a great deal to consider and compare with the existing law. There are some similarities, but also a great deal of change which will need to be known. As yet we have little or no guidance as to how the Act will work in practice; no doubt we shall soon have enough to ponder.